German Intonation

AN OUTLINE

German Intonation

AN OUTLINE

Anthony Fox

CLARENDON PRESS · OXFORD
1984

Oxford University Press, Walton Street, Oxford OX2 6DP

London New York Toronto
Delhi Bombay Calcutta Madras Karachi
Kuala Lumpur Singapore Hong Kong Tokyo
Nairobi Dar es Salaam Cape Town
Melbourne Auckland

and associates in

Beirut Berlin Ibadan Mexico City Nicosia

Oxford is a trade mark of Oxford University Press

Published in the United States
by Oxford University Press, New York

British Library Cataloguing in Publication Data

Fox, Anthony
German intonation.
1. German language – Intonation
I. Title
431.6   PF3139
ISBN 0-19-815794-0

Library of Congress Cataloging in Publication Data
Fox, Anthony.
German intonation.
Bibliography: p.
Includes index.
1. German language – Intonation.   I. Title.
PF3139.5.F6 1984   431'.6   83-24399
ISBN 0-19-815794-0

Set by Hope Services, Abingdon
Printed in Great Britain by Billings & Sons Ltd,
Worcester

Preface

Compared with the considerable body of writing on English intonation, the available literature on German intonation is relatively sparse, and much of it is inaccessible to students, either because, being written in German, it overtaxes their competence in the language, or because it demands more theoretical sophistication in linguistics than the student possesses, or indeed would need to possess. Furthermore, few works consider in detail the differences and similarities between the intonation systems of the two languages, or make explicit reference to the problems of the English-speaking learner. There are honourable exceptions, such as W. G. Moulton's *The Sounds of English and German*, or P. A. D. MacCarthy's *The Pronunciation of German*, but these are only brief chapters in books which deal with wider issues. The last full-length book to pursue such aims – Marie Barker's *A Handbook of German Intonation* – was published over half a century ago.

It is to remedy this lack that the present book has been written. I have attempted to explain the major features of German intonation for the benefit of English-speaking learners in a way which will not make excessive demands on their command of German or their acquaintance with linguistic theory. It is not, therefore, primarily a theoretical work, and I have deliberately kept discussion of theoretical issues to a minimum, and made little reference to alternative analyses. For the same reason I have not given a full bibliographical apparatus, as this would be alien to the essentially introductory character of the book. Instead, I have given suggestions for further reading, in which a number of the major contributions to the study of German and English intonation are included.

Fellow workers in this field, and those familiar with the scholarly literature on the subject – the book is, of course, not primarily addressed to them – will no doubt find much to question or to disagree with. In view of the complexity of the subject-matter, the absence of any agreed orthodoxy in the manner of its description, and the elementary nature of the book, this could hardly be otherwise, and it demands no apology. But I hope that such readers might also find something of interest and relevance for their own work.

The book has arisen from many years of preoccupation with German intonation and from attempts to explain it to students of the language. Its findings are based largely on my own research into the subject. But it will also be evident that I owe a great debt to my predecessors in the analysis of intonation. In its general approach, the book owes much to the British tradition of intonation description, which is exemplified in the works of Harold Palmer, Lilias Armstrong and Ida Ward, Roger Kingdon, Maria Schubiger, J. D. O'Connor and G. F. Arnold, and Michael Halliday, among others, and which also underlies the work on German of John Trim and John Pheby. In common with others working in the field of intonation, I have a special obligation to the writings of Michael Halliday, whose influence will be discernible throughout the book.

A different, though no less significant debt I owe to those who have been of more practical assistance in the preparation of this work. To Hanno Martin, who offered encouragement and helpful comments on the manuscript; to Joan Colman, whose feats of decipherment in rendering the manuscript into typewritten form rival those of Champollion; and especially to my family, who experienced the ups and downs of this work through my own distracted behaviour; to all of these I offer my sincere thanks.

Leeds, April 1983   ANTHONY FOX

Contents

1
Introduction

THE IMPORTANCE OF INTONATION

It is a common experience in learning to pronounce a foreign language to find that although we may have mastered the individual sounds of the language we still fail to sound like a native speaker. Some elusive quality, peculiar to the language in question, seems to be lacking. The elements that make up this quality are not always easy to identify, and they may be still more difficult to imitate. They include the way in which sounds are combined together in speech, details of accentuation and stress, peculiarities of rhythm and the length of individual sounds and syllables, and, on a larger scale, the particular 'voice quality' which speakers of the language habitually use.

But one major characteristic in which languages may differ and which contributes to their distinctive sound is undoubtedly their *intonation*, the patterns of voice pitch and the way in which they are used. Although the basic features of the use of voice pitch may be broadly similar in many languages, each language nevertheless has its own particular usages, and differences will often be found to exist even among different groups of speakers of the same language. Our use of intonation in our own language has become so instinctive and natural to us that we are generally completely unaware of it, and we fail to make the necessary adjustments when speaking a foreign language. The result is that however convincing our articulation of individual sounds may be, we betray our origins in every sentence that we utter.

We may of course question the necessity of acquiring a perfect pronunciation of a foreign language. After all, the main objective must surely be intelligibility, and the capacity to *communicate* as efficiently as the native speaker in the language in question. The ability to pass for a native speaker is undoubtedly a desirable accomplishment for those who can acquire it, but it is hardly an essential one, except perhaps for those who wish to take up espionage as a career. But intonation is not just a meaningless accompaniment to speech; as we shall see in later chapters, it is *meaningful*, and has considerable *communicative* significance. Communication may therefore be impaired if the foreign learner of a language fails to detect, or to interpret correctly, those aspects of the speaker's meaning that are conveyed by intonation, or if he fails to give appropriate expression to his own meaning in his intonation when speaking the foreign language.

THE PROBLEMS OF INTONATION

Intonation is thus an area of the pronunciation of a language which the foreign learner must endeavour to master if he is to have the communicative ability of the native speaker. But how is this to be achieved? In intonation, as in other areas of language, there are undoubtedly some learners who are able to 'pick up', often unconsciously, the features of the foreign language. But many learners are not able to do this; they must be *taught* the features of the language, have them brought to their attention and be given practice in their use.

We are immediately confronted by a difficulty here. For features of a language to be taught it is necessary for the teacher to know the 'facts' that he is teaching. But the major problem with intonation is that the 'facts' are remarkably difficult to establish. Although, in using their own language, speakers respond immediately and instinctively to the meaning conveyed by other people's intonation and are able to convey their own meaning effortlessly in the same way, it is extremely difficult for them to identify this meaning or to isolate the features of the intonation pattern that are being used to convey it.

This difficulty is not restricted to 'naïve' speakers but is shared by scholars who make a special study of intonation. Thus, works on the intonation of individual languages differ considerably in what they take the 'facts' of the intonation of the language in question to be. While it would be unusual for books dealing with, say, the verbs of a language to differ materially in the forms that they described or in the basic meanings that they gave to them, such variability is the norm rather than the exception in intonation studies. This state of affairs presents both teacher and learner with special problems, since they are not sure what they should be teaching or learning.

Why should intonation present problems of this kind? As we shall see in later chapters, the cause lies in the nature of intonation itself. Intonation cannot be easily reduced, in the manner of 'declensions' of the noun or 'conjugations' of the verb, to a simple set of 'forms' each with a specific identifiable meaning. The structure of intonation is complex, with different pitch features superimposed upon one another, and we cannot cut up the pitch pattern into neat segments or isolate forms clearly from one another. Its meaning is frustratingly difficult to pin down, and is different in kind from that associated with individual words or grammatical constructions. All this leads to considerable uncertainty in the analysis of the intonation of a language, and, as a result, no description can really lay claim to being 'correct' in the sense that it is the only satisfactory or legitimate approach to intonation patterns and their uses. It is possible to view intonation in various ways, and to analyse and describe it according to different principles.

These reservations apply equally well to the present book. It cannot be properly claimed that this book presents the 'facts' of German intonation in the sense in which this term is normally understood. This is not to say that the statements contained in it are believed to be untrue, but simply that the analysis given here is simply one way of looking at the phenomena concerned, and other approaches might be equally valid. To make stronger claims than this would be dishonest and misleading in view of the present state of intonation studies.

What this book attempts to do is to present an approach to the intonational features of German which, it is hoped, will enable the English-speaking learner to appreciate more fully the role that they play in spoken German, and to come closer to his goal of possessing the native speaker's communicative ability in this area of the language.

WHOSE INTONATION?

A further problem arises here which is not peculiar to intonation. We have already noted that languages may differ in their intonation, and that even within a single language there may be variation between different speakers. This applies, of course, to other aspects of pronunciation and, to a more limited extent, to grammar and vocabulary, too. The difficulty for the foreign learner is that of choosing the particular form of the language that he should learn. It is usual, and natural, for most foreign learners to attempt to acquire mastery of the 'standard' form of the language as opposed to a regional dialect, since it has wider currency and is more acceptable for the majority of purposes. But though the standard is generally fairly homogeneous in matters of grammar and vocabulary, its pronunciation may vary within rather wider limits, resulting in a number of regional 'accents'. The choice of an appropriate accent is not necessarily an obvious one for the foreign learner.

In the case of German we may identify without difficulty a standard language which is valid throughout the German-speaking area for official and cultural purposes, and for the everyday usage of most educated speakers. This form is generally known as *Hochdeutsch*, and it is contrasted with *Dialekt* or *Mundart*. It is less easy to identify a 'standard' pronunciation of *Hochdeutsch*, however. On the whole, apart from a number of characteristic regional features, it is North German forms that have the most prestige, and which can therefore serve as a model for learners. The somewhat artificial pronunciation advocated by Siebs in his *Deutsche Hochsprache*, which is often taken as authoritative, is basically Northern in type, despite its claims to being non-regional.

The adoption of a Northern type of pronunciation can reasonably be extended to features of intonation, too. There are certainly differences in the intonation of speakers from different parts of the German-speaking area. The German phonetician Eduard Sievers suggested that North and South German intonations are like 'mirror images' of each other: where the pitch rises in one, it falls in the other, and vice versa. This is no doubt an exaggeration, but it is certainly true that regional differences may be quite noticeable. Nevertheless, it is legitimate to claim that a learner who has mastered North German forms may use them everywhere without embarrassment and without fear of being seriously misunderstood. The intonation described in this book is therefore of a Northern type.

VARIETIES OF ENGLISH INTONATION

The variety of pronunciations found within German is of course paralleled by a similar kind of variety within English. In this book, which is specifically intended for English-speakers, it has often been found useful to make comparisons between German and English intonation in order to identify the particular difficulties encountered by native speakers of English learning German. The variety of English intonation naturally makes such comparisons difficult, indeed potentially misleading. As far as possible, the features of English intonation presented here are those which are known to be characteristic of a large number of speakers, particularly within England, and which have been described in some detail in works on English intonation. (These works deal largely with the accent known as 'Received Pronunciation', but are in fact more widely applicable.)

It is almost certain, however, that some features described as characteristic of 'English' will in fact not occur in the pronunciation of some readers of this book. It is essential, therefore, that the reader should constantly check the assertions made about English intonation against his own usage. This is in any case valuable, not simply in order to avoid misunderstandings as to the nature of the problems to be overcome, but because it induces the practice of observing one's own intonation, of bringing to the level of conscious awareness one's own unconscious speech habits. For many learners, this 'monitoring' of existing speech habits, whether or not they conform to the remarks made in this book, will be a necessary, or at least useful, prerequisite for the acquisition of new ones.

2
The Structure of German Intonation

PITCH

Intonation can be described as the use of *voice pitch* in speech. When we speak, our vocal cords — two bands of ligament in the larynx at the top of the windpipe — vibrate rapidly, alternately opening and closing the air passage, and thus producing the sound which we call *voice*. The rate at which they vibrate gives this sound that particular characteristic which we call its *pitch*.

Although we are not normally conscious of doing so, we are able to control with considerable accuracy the rate at which the vocal cords vibrate and thus to vary the pitch: the faster the vibration, the *higher* the pitch; the slower the vibration, the *lower* the pitch. This results in a *scale* of pitch from low to high.

Such a 'scale' differs from a musical scale in a number of respects. A musical scale consists of a definite number of notes in a fixed relationship to one another, and with specific steps, or intervals, between them. The pitch scale of speech is *continuous*, with no fixed notes or intervals; we cannot speak 'out of tune'. Nor, since the pitch range of individual speakers varies, can we speak 'in the wrong key'; 'high' and 'low' pitch are always relative, depending on the range of the speaker's voice.

Any piece of speech will be spoken with a continuously changing pitch, and the pitch pattern produced can be called its *intonation*. With a little practice, even without particular musical gifts, it is possible for most people to hear the pitch pattern of utterances and to write it down. The standard musical notation is, for the reasons just mentioned, unsuitable for the recording of intonation patterns; it is more satisfactory to indicate the normal limits of the speaker's pitch range by two parallel lines and to draw a continuous line between them to indicate the pitch:

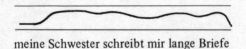

meine Schwester schreibt mir lange Briefe

Such a notation is not as helpful as it might be, as it is difficult to relate specific parts of the intonation pattern to individual words and syllables. For ease of reading, therefore, we may use a broken line, where each dash corresponds to a syllable:

meine Schwester schreibt mir lange Briefe

Or, more helpful still, we may represent stressed or accented syllables by lines, and unstressed or unaccented syllables by dots:

meine Schwester schreibt mir lange Briefe

We do not actually speak with breaks between the syllables in this way, of course; the pitch pattern of an utterance is auditorily continuous. Each of the above three examples represents the same intonation pattern, the differences being simply in the way we choose to represent it on paper. The last two versions make the pattern somewhat easier to read by allowing us to relate the various parts of the pattern to individual words and syllables.

The pitch pattern of utterances is not arbitrary but systematic; it follows set principles in consistent and meaningful ways. In particular the intonation has a certain *structure*: it has various components which fit together. The remainder of this chapter will consider the nature of this structure and of the principles on which it is based.

ACCENTS

Of considerable importance for the intonation patterns of German is the *accentual structure* of the utterance. In any German utterance certain syllables stand out as being particularly prominent, and these can be described as *accented* (stressed). In the above example, the syllables *Schwes-*, *schreibt*, *lang-*, and *Brief-* are the accented syllables. Accented syllables form the foundation, so to speak, of the intonation pattern, and the pattern is largely built upon them. It is therefore important to be able to identify the accented syllables in any utterance. There are, furthermore, different degrees of prominence that accented syllables may have. Of the accented syllables in this example the syllable *Brief-* stands out as being especially prominent. We shall therefore distinguish between *primary accents* (*Brief-*) and *secondary accents* (*Schwes-*, *schreibt*, *lang-*). Again, this distinction is an important one for intonation, as the pitch pattern associated with primary accents is the key to the structure of the intonation of German utterances.

THE NUCLEUS

Every utterance, however short, must have at least one syllable with a primary accent. The basic and most significant part of the intonation pattern of an utterance is found in or near those syllables which have a primary accent. To appreciate the importance of primary accents for intonation, consider the following examples:

1.   das Buch hat zehn **Mark** gekostet

2.   warum hast du meinen **Brief** nicht gelesen?

3.   haben Sie meinen **Hund** gesehen?

In all these cases, the syllable which has the primary accent is in bold type. If we examine the intonation patterns given here (these are merely examples of appropriate intonations, and there are many others) we see that the primary accent is associated with a *noticeable pitch change*: in examples (1) and (2) the syllable with the primary accent has a high pitch immediately followed by a jump down to a low pitch, while in example (3) the syllable with the primary accent is the first syllable with a low pitch after a sequence of high-pitched syllables, and it forms the start of a rising sequence of syllables. Thus, one of the characteristics of a syllable which has a primary accent is that it has a prominent place in the pitch pattern of the utterance, though this prominence may be achieved by various means. In fact, it is the prominence given to this syllable by its place in the pitch pattern that is one of the chief clues by which we recognize that it is a syllable with a primary accent.

The syllable with the primary accent forms the centre or core of the intonation pattern. The term that we shall use for this is *nucleus*. In the above examples, the words *Mark*, *Brief*, and *Hund* thus occur at the nucleus of the intonation pattern of their respective utterances. In utterances with more than one primary accent, each syllable with such an accent will occur at the nucleus of an intonation pattern. There is one nucleus for every primary accent.

THE INTONATION GROUP

It can be seen, therefore, that the intonation of an utterance is divided up into sections by the number of primary accents, and hence the number of nuclei, it contains: there are as many intonation patterns within the utterance as there are nuclei. Each such section, or pattern, which contains a nucleus we may call an *intonation group*. The intonation of any utterance therefore consists of one, or more than one, intonation group, with one nucleus in each. The only exception to this is where, in colloquial speech, the speaker is interrupted, changes his mind, forgets what he is going to say, etc. This may result in incomplete intonation groups.

An intonation group can be of any length, though longer utterances will generally be split up into several groups (see chapter 13, below). The following examples, which differ in length and in grammatical complexity, could all be spoken as single intonation groups:

ja
ich **weiß**
er ist **ges**tern gekommen
ich weiß nicht, ob er **ges**tern gekommen ist

In these examples, the syllable with the primary accent, and at which the nucleus occurs, is in bold type. Again, this is just one possibility among several; apart from the first example, which consists of only a single syllable, these utterances could also have the nucleus elsewhere (see chapter 8, below).

THE STRUCTURE OF THE INTONATION GROUP

As we have seen, every utterance contains one or more intonation groups, each with a nucleus. In utterances consisting of a single syllable, such as *ja*, *nein*, *schön*, etc., the nucleus is, of course, all that occurs, but in the majority of intonation groups there will be other syllables, too. The nucleus can in principle occur anywhere in the intonation group (see chapter 8, below). If it is at the beginning, then there will be a part of the intonation group *after* the nucleus; if it is at the end, then there will be part of the intonation group *before* the nucleus; and if it is in the middle there will be a part *before* and a part *after*.

The following examples illustrate these possibilities:

1.   nucleus alone:

nein

2.   nucleus at the beginning:

Hans war hier

3.   nucleus at the end:

frag mal den **Hans**!

4.   nucleus in the middle:

ich habe den **Hans** gesehen

There are thus three parts to the intonation group. In addition to the nucleus, which must be present in every intonation group, there is a part which may precede it, called the *head*, and a part which may follow it, called the *tail*. Example (4) could therefore be analysed as follows:

head	nucleus	tail
ich habe den	**Hans**	gesehen

The basic structure given here for German intonation, with an inton-ation group consisting of head, nucleus, and tail, is equally applicable to English. In learning German, therefore, speakers of English do not have to learn a new kind of intonation structure. As we shall see in later chapters, the differences between the intonation systems of the two languages lie not in the basic structure of the patterns but in their pitch, *and in the way in which the patterns are used.*

3
Nuclear Patterns

We saw in the last chapter that the intonation group can consist of three parts: head, nucleus, and tail, and that of these the nucleus is the most important. Though the head and the tail may be lacking, there is always a nucleus, and it is the pitch pattern of the nucleus that gives to the intonation group its basic character and meaning. For the description of the pitch pattern, it is in fact best to take the nucleus and tail together; the tail is little more than an appendix to the nucleus, and it is the combined pitch of nucleus and tail that we need to consider. This combined pitch pattern, including both the nucleus and the tail, can be called the *nuclear pattern*.

In this chapter we shall consider the basic kinds of nuclear pattern that can occur in German. The fundamental distinction that must be made is between patterns which *end high* and patterns which *end low*. In the former the final pitch reached by the pattern is relatively high within the speaker's range, while in the latter the final pitch is relatively low. This distinction is of considerable importance for the function of the patterns, as will be seen in later chapters. Each of these types appears in various different forms.

LOW-ENDING PATTERNS

We may distinguish two basic types of low-ending pattern. Both of these have a final low pitch, but they differ in the first part of the pattern. These two types are the *fall* and the *rise–fall*.

1. The falling pattern

The basic and most common low-ending pattern has a *falling* pitch. The pattern starts relatively high and drops, usually quite rapidly, to a low pitch. Here are some examples (the nucleus is in bold type):

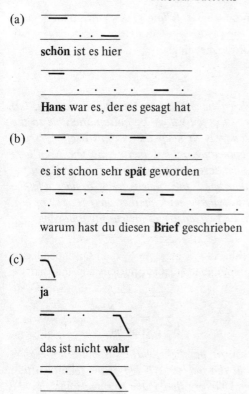

(a)

schön ist es hier

Hans war es, der es gesagt hat

(b)

es ist schon sehr spät geworden

warum hast du diesen Brief geschrieben

(c)

ja

das ist nicht wahr

wo ist mein Hut?

As can be seen, all these examples end in a low pitch, and they are all therefore instances of low-ending patterns. It will also be observed that the nucleus begins at a relatively high pitch and there must therefore be a *fall* at some point in the pattern, either during or immediately after the syllable which has the nucleus. If there is no head, as in the examples of (a), with the nucleus at the beginning of the intonation group, then the nucleus itself is at a *high-level* pitch, and is followed by a *jump down* to a low-pitched tail. The same pattern is found if the nucleus is in the middle of the intonation group, as in the examples of (b); here the high pitch of the head is continued by the nucleus, but there is immediately a jump down to the low pitch of the tail.

In the examples of (c) there is no tail, and here the pattern differs slightly. Instead of a high-pitched nucleus with a jump down to a low-pitched tail, both the high and the low pitch are incorporated into the nucleus itself, producing a *falling glide* rather than a jump down. This difference is simply the result of the absence of a tail, and is of no significance for the meaning.

English has a pattern which is analogous to the fall of German, but there are slight differences of detail which are quite noticeable to the ear. In German the tendency is to keep the nucleus itself high and level with a falling glide appearing only if there is no tail. Even here the nucleus begins with a high-level pitch and falls fairly rapidly at the end. In English, on the other hand, the nucleus tends to have a falling glide throughout the nuclear syllable, and whether there is a tail or not. Compare typical forms for the two languages such as the following:

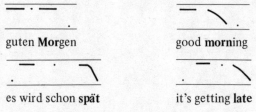

guten **Morgen**	good **morn**ing

| es wird schon **spät** | it's getting **late** |

This difference may appear to be slight, but it is quite noticeable. The sustained high pitch in the nuclear syllable of the falling pattern in German is one of several factors that make German sound, to the English ear at least, rather vigorous and emphatic. English-speakers may imitate this by ensuring that the nuclear syllable is pronounced as far as possible with a high-level pitch *in all cases, and by keeping falling glides to a minimum.*

2. *The rising-falling pattern*

The rising-falling pattern is less important and less frequent than the falling pattern, but it has a quite distinctive function. Though it, too, ends in a low pitch, it also can begin fairly low, and first rises then falls. The pitch of the nucleus itself again depends on the presence or absence of a tail, and also upon the number of syllables that the tail contains. Here are some examples:

(a)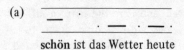

schön ist das Wetter heute

(b)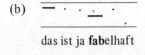

das ist ja **fab**elhaft

(c)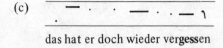

das hat er doch wieder ver**ges**sen

(d)

ich **weiß**   **nein**

As can be seen, the basic shape is the same in all cases: a rise followed by a fall. But the exact form of this pattern depends on the number of syllables over which it is spread. With three or more syllables in the nuclear pattern, as in examples (a) and (b), the nucleus itself has a mid or low pitch, and it is followed by a high and then a low-pitched syllable. With two syllables in the nuclear pattern, as in example (c), the high and final low pitch are combined into a falling glide on the final syllable. (Since this syllable is unaccented, a *thin* line is used to represent the glide rather than the thick one used for accented syllables.) In the examples of (d), where there is no tail at all, both the rise and the fall are concentrated in the single syllable of the nucleus, though again the nuclear syllable starts level.

It will be clear that the main difference between the falling and the rising-falling patterns is in the short rising movement before the final fall. This rise generally takes place on an unaccented syllable, and need not be very large, so that in some cases the distinction between the two types of low-ending pattern is not very marked. In fact, they merge into each other without a clear boundary between them (see also chapter 4).

An analogous pattern, with similarly different forms according to the number of syllables, is found in English. As with the simple falling pattern, however, English prefers glides *to* jumps, *so that the pattern is* curved *rather than* stepped. *The following examples illustrate typical English forms with three, two, and one syllable in the nuclear pattern respectively:*

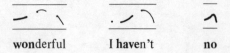

wonderful   **I haven**'t   **no**

The overall shape is the same as the German, but the pitch changes are smoother and more gradual.

If we compare the forms of both the low-ending patterns in the two languages it is evident that they differ in the same way in each case. With both the fall and the rise–fall German prefers level pitches with jumps between them, while English has more glides, whether rising or falling. Thus, the languages differ here not in the basic forms or patterns that they use but rather in the manner in which the pitch changes. *Rather than attempt to learn details of the individual forms, the English learner should try to cultivate this way of changing the pitch, jumping rather than gliding up or down. This should result in acceptable forms of both the low-ending patterns.*

HIGH-ENDING PATTERNS

High-ending patterns have a final high pitch. Two main types may be distinguished according to the shape of the pattern: the *rising* and the *level* patterns. In the former there is a preceding low pitch which rises at the end, while in the latter the pitch remains relatively high throughout.

1. *The rising pattern*

The basic and most frequent high-ending pattern is the *rise*. This is in many respects the reverse of the fall: in its simplest form the nucleus begins at a relatively low pitch and the final pitch reached by the nuclear pattern is high within the speaker's range. Here are some examples:

(a)

wie bitte?   **kommt** er denn?

(b)

wie **spät** ist es?   hast du meinen **Hut** gesehen?

(c)   ja   was?   jetzt

(d)   haben Sie das ge**wußt**?   bist du schon **da**?

In the examples of (a) and (b) there is a tail following the nucleus, and the nucleus itself is low and level. An important difference between this pattern and the comparable form of the falling pattern is that the pitch change is spread out over the whole tail rather than taking place in a sudden jump immediately after the nucleus. The tail starts low, and each successive syllable has a slightly higher pitch. There is generally rather greater movement on the final syllable, which forms a rising glide. The rise on each syllable of the tail depends on the length of the tail as a whole: the shorter the tail, the greater the rise must be on each syllable in order to finish at a high pitch.

The examples of (c) and (d) have no tail at all. Here the rise to the final high pitch must take place in the nucleus itself. In this case the nucleus begins with a low-level pitch, but has a rapid rising glide at the end.

A further comment must be made about the examples of (b) and (d), in which there is a head preceding the nucleus. The head is at a high pitch, but the nucleus must begin low; there must therefore be a jump down before the start of the nucleus. This jump down is exactly the same as that occurring *after* the nucleus with the falling nuclear pattern where there is a tail, but its status is quite different. With the rising pattern the jump down before the nucleus is merely a transition between the end of the high head and the beginning of the nucleus; it is not a distinctive part of the pattern, and it disappears if there is no head (or if the head is low – see chapter 5). But with the falling pattern the pitch change to low is an intrinsic and necessary part of the pattern which does not disappear in the absence of a head. This is a good illustration of how similar pitch features may often be interpreted quite differently according to where they are used and according to their structural role within the intonation group.

How, then, do we know, on hearing the jump down, whether it is the transitional fall of the rising pattern or the intrinsic fall of the falling pattern? In fact, it is only through the tail that we are able to distinguish them. In the falling pattern the tail remains low and level until the end of the intonation group, while in the rising pattern the tail gradually rises, reaching a high pitch at the end, e.g.

fall:

er **kommt** morgen wieder

rise:

er kommt **mor**gen wieder

The first three syllables would here be ambiguous: the pattern could be either a falling pattern with the nucleus on *kommt*, or a rising pattern with the nucleus on *morgen*. The ambiguity is resolved by the pitch of the tail. This also shows that, although the nucleus is the most important part of the intonation group, it is nevertheless the nuclear pattern *as a whole* which conveys the distinctive pitch features. The tail is not necessarily dispensable.

In fact, the ambiguity here is still more serious than this example would suggest. We shall see in the next chapter that yet another interpretation of the pitch pattern of this utterance is possible, namely as a falling–rising variant of the rising pattern. In many cases only the context can resolve the ambiguity: in a specific case the context will suggest where the nucleus is likely to be located (see chapter 8, below), and the pattern is interpreted in the light of this expectation. Thus, in the present example, in a given context we might expect the nucleus to be on *kommt* rather than *morgen*, and this would allow us to identify the pattern as a fall rather than a rise even before the tail is heard.

English has a comparable pattern which does not differ appreciably from the German rise. In both languages the nucleus is low and level if there is a tail, but forms a rising glide if there is none. As in the case of the fall and the rise-fall, however, there is a tendency for the pitch changes to be more gradual and less abrupt than in German, but the difference is less noticeable here than with the low-ending forms. Examples are:

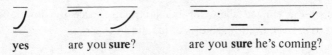

| yes | are you **sure**? | are you **sure** he's coming? |

2. *The level pattern*

A further, more restricted high-ending pattern is basically *high* and *level* throughout. It is especially common as a non-final pattern, i.e. where it is followed by another intonation group, but it can also occur independently, especially in short utterances:

(a)

gut   **schön**

(b)

danke schön

regnet es . . . (so können wir nicht ausgehen)

(c)

ja**wohl**   wenn du **willst** . . . (komme ich mit)

wenn du morgen **kommst** . . . (fahren wir zusammen)

(d)

falls es morgen **reg**nen sollte . . . (so können wir nicht ausgehen)

It will be noticed that the pitch of the nucleus is the same, whether there is a tail, as in (b) and (d), or none, as in (a) and (c). The tail simply continues the high level pitch of the nucleus. Where there is a head, as in the examples of (c) and (d), an important characteristic of this pattern is the *jump up* to the high level pitch of the nucleus. The nucleus must always be at a higher pitch than the immediately preceding syllable. If the preceding head is high, its pitch must fall towards the end to allow for the jump up, hence the lower pitch given to *morgen* in the examples of (c) and (d).

English-speakers can *use a level pattern of similar form to the German one, but they do so only rarely. In German, however, this pattern is quite frequent, and its use must be cultivated by the English learner. For many Germans this pattern is the normal one in intonation groups which are non-final, whereas English-speakers prefer to use other patterns for this purpose (see chapter 7, below).*

NOTATION

The dot and line notation which we have used in giving the details of the various patterns is too cumbersome for describing the inton-ation of whole texts. For this purpose it is more convenient to in-corporate the indication of the intonation into the normal written form of the utterances by using intonation marks. Since the nucleus of the intonation pattern occurs in a syllable which has a primary accent (see p. 8 above), we may use an accent mark to indicate the nuclear pattern. For example, the mark ` placed before a syllable indicates that this syllable is the nucleus of the intonation group, and that the nuclear pattern of this intonation group is *falling*. The utterance:

guten **Mor**gen

can therefore be represented simply as *guten `Morgen*. By following the principles set out above with regard to the structure of the individual nu-clear patterns it is easy to convert this back into the visual representation with dots and lines: in the falling pattern, the nucleus itself has a high pitch, and the tail a low pitch, hence the syllable *Mor-* will be high and the syllable *-gen* low. Similar procedures can be followed with the other accent marks.

The accent marks used in this book are as follows:

1. *Low-ending patterns*

   (a) *falling:*   `
       example: `heute

heute

(b) *rising–falling:* ˆ
    example: ˆheute

heute

2. *High-ending patterns*

(a) *rising:* ´
    example: ´heute

heute

(b) *level:* ‐
    example: ‐heute

heute

4
Variants of the Nuclear Patterns

The four nuclear patterns described in the previous chapter may be regarded as the basic ones that occur in German. They do not, however, always appear in the same form; each of them has a range of variation, and the choice of a particular variant form is significant for the meaning. Roughly speaking, we may say that the variant forms of a particular pattern differ from one another in the impression of 'strength' or 'emphasis' that they give: there are 'stronger' and 'weaker', or 'emphatic' and 'unemphatic' forms of the same nuclear pattern. The precise significance of this variation for the meaning will be considered in more detail in chapter 10, below. For the moment we are concerned only with the different pitch patterns themselves.

VARIANTS OF THE FALLING PATTERN

Variant forms of the falling nuclear pattern differ from one another primarily in the *height* of the start of the fall. We have seen that in this pattern the nucleus is basically high and level, with either a jump down to a low tail or, in the absence of a tail, a falling glide within the nuclear syllable itself. The height of the level pitch of the nucleus may vary, ranging from the top to the bottom of the speaker's range. The higher the pitch of the nucleus, the 'stronger' the impression given. The following are typical forms:

high: ___ ·   mid: ___ ·   low: — ·

      danke   **dan**ke   **dan**ke

In the 'high' form the nucleus is relatively high within the speaker's range, but in the 'mid' form the pitch is somewhat lower. In both cases there is a characteristic jump (or glide) down to the final low pitch. The 'low' form is different; here the nucleus itself is at a low pitch, and the tail, if there is one, merely continues this pitch until the end of the intonation group. The falling nature of this form is, of course, not actually evident from the nuclear pattern itself, since the pitch is low throughout.

The low form is, in fact, another instance of an ambiguous pattern, where knowledge of the position of the nucleus is crucial for identification. If this form follows a high-pitched head, then the pitch pattern will be exactly the same as that found with a high or mid variant of the fall where the nucleus is on the preceding syllable. Thus *ich `weiß es* with the nucleus on *weiß* and the low variant of the fall is identical in its pitch pattern to *`ich weiß es* with the nucleus on *ich* and the high or mid variant of the fall:

<table>
<tr><td>

ich **weiß** es</td><td>

ich weiß es</td></tr>
</table>

The two utterances may not be completely identical, as the different position of the primary accent may bring with it differences in the relative prominence of the individual syllables, as well as a different rhythm, but in many cases they will indeed be indistinguishable, and the context may be the only way of resolving the ambiguity which results.

Pitch height is, of course, a relative matter, and the distinction between the 'high' and 'mid' variants must therefore be seen in relation not only to the habitual pitch range of the speaker but also to the range of the individual utterance. A clue to the interpretation of a particular form may be provided by the height of the preceding head, which can give a frame of reference. Thus in example (a), the pitch of the nucleus may be judged 'mid' because it does not rise above that of the end of the head, while the same pitch in (b) may be interpreted as 'high' since there is a jump up from the end of the head:

(a)   (b)

ich bin **müde**   ich bin **müde**

In all these cases it is extremely important to note that differences of pitch height are not a matter of a limited number of separate steps but form a *continuous scale*. The 'high', 'mid', and 'low' variants given here are not absolute, but simply convenient points on this scale to which we may give names. Forms may begin at *any* height within the speaker's range. The existence of such continuous variation rather than simply a fixed set of alternatives is one of the most characteristic and most important features of intonation. While the majority of other areas of language allow only a choice between a specified number of alternative forms (different words, grammatical forms, syntactic constructions, etc.) intonation allows an indefinite number of alternatives on a sliding scale.

The kind of variation described here, with a scale of pitch height for the nucleus, is also found in English, though with the characteristic glides of the English fall:

high: mid: low:

     I **have**n't   I **have**n't   I **have**n't

The difference between the typically gliding fall of English and the typically jumping fall of German naturally disappears in the low form, where there is no fall at all.

VARIANTS OF THE RISING-FALLING PATTERN

Similar varieties, differing in apparent 'strength', are found with the rising-falling pattern. As with the variants of the fall, 'strong' forms have a wider range and 'weak' forms are narrower, but since this pattern begins mid or low rather than high this variation is manifested somewhat differently. Wide forms tend to have a lower nuclear syllable and they reach a higher pitch in the rising part of the pattern, while in narrow forms there is far less pitch movement and the nucleus does not start so low. The following are typical forms:

wide: mid: narrow:

     fabelhaft!   **fa**belhaft!   **fa**belhaft!

    The 'weak' end of the range of forms (again it is a scale and not a set of separate forms) tends to become more and more like the simple falling pattern as the rising phase becomes narrower. Indeed, the first syllable of the tail may be at the same pitch as the nucleus, with no rise at all. The distinction between the two low-ending patterns, the rise-fall and the fall, is in fact not an absolute one. Like the variant forms of each of these patterns, the patterns themselves are not necessarily neatly separable from each other and may have no clear line of demarcation. Although it is convenient to see them as separate patterns with distinct meanings, neither in form nor in meaning can we say at what point one gives way to the other.

A similar range of forms is found with the English rising-falling pattern, though again with a gliding rather than jumping tendency. As with the German form, the English rise-fall cannot be clearly delimited from the simple fall:

wide: ‾‾‾‾ ⌐   mid: ‾‾‾‾ ⌐   narrow: ‾‾‾‾ ⌐
wonderful   **won**derful   **won**derful

VARIANTS OF THE RISING PATTERN

The rising pattern also has a range of variation, though the differences here are not just a matter of pitch height or range. The form described in the previous chapter, with a rising shape beginning low and ending high, may be regarded as basic, while other forms are 'stronger' or 'weaker'. The high ending is characteristic of *all* forms of the rising pattern; 'weaker' forms are obtained by starting somewhat less low, thus reducing the overall range. Since the basic form starts at the bottom of the speaker's range, 'stronger' forms cannot be produced simply by extending the range. Instead, the falling transition to the low pitch with which the rising pattern starts is postponed, so that the nuclear syllable itself is *high* rather than low. This results in a falling-rising shape rather than a simple rise:

fall-rise: ‾‾‾ ⌐   wide rise: ‾‾‾ ⌐   narrow rise: ‾‾‾ ⌐
heute   **heu**te   **heu**te

Within the fall-rise type, further gradations can be obtained by varying the height of the nucleus:

high: ‾‾‾ ⌐   mid: ‾‾‾ ⌐
heute   **heu**te

(A fall-rise pattern commencing with a *low* nuclear syllable would, of course, be the same as the simple wide rise.)

As noted in the previous chapter, the rise in these patterns takes place throughout the tail, but where there is no tail the rise is in the nuclear syllable itself. In the case of the fall–rise variety, this means that the high initial pitch, the fall to the low start of the rise, and the rise itself, may all be concentrated into a single syllable:

ist es **schön**?　　　　　　　ist er schon **da**?

With the fall–rise form, too, ambiguity can arise with regard to the position of the nucleus. An intonation group with a falling-rising pattern may have an identical pitch pattern to an intonation group in which a simple rising nuclear pattern is preceded by a high head. Thus *sind ˇSie müde?* (the mark ˇ indicates the falling-rising variant) could be indistinguishable from *sind Sie ´mude?*.

fall–rise: ＿＿＿＿＿＿＿＿　　rise: ＿＿＿＿＿＿＿＿
　　　　　sind **Sie** müde?　　　　　　sind Sie **mü**de?

Again features of prominence or rhythm may serve to differentiate them in many cases, though the context may often be needed to resolve the ambiguity.

As with the variants of the other patterns, these different forms are simply points on a *continuous scale*, which extends from the 'strong' high fall–rise form to the 'weak' narrow rise. Although we may for convenience divide this scale into separate forms, it is not possible to draw clear boundaries between them.

The English rising pattern is also subject to a similar kind of variation, though there are other factors to be taken into account here, too. A 'stronger' falling-rising form and a 'weaker' narrow form may be recognized in addition to the basic wide rising variety:

fall–rise: ＿＿＿　　wide rise: ＿＿＿　　narrow rise: ＿＿＿
has he?　　　　　　**has** he?　　　　　　**has** he?

The only significant difference between the two languages here is in the treatment of the falling phase of the falling-rising variant. While the German form usually has a high-level nucleus followed by a jump down to the low start of the rise, the English form generally has a glide down. This is, of course, exactly parallel to the difference between the German and English forms of the simple fall, and we have observed analogous differences with the other nuclear patterns.

There are some further complications here, however, since English has a number of other patterns which are not found in German and which are superficially similar to those just described. One of these may be called the rise–fall–rise *(though in a 'weaker' form the first part may be level rather than rising). This pattern is rather similar to the fall–rise but differs from it in important respects. Its pitch is generally lower than that of the falling–rising pattern, and the various pitch changes which take place within it are more gradual. The following examples illustrate these differences:*

fall–rise: do you **think** so?   rise–fall–rise: I **think** so

This rising–falling–rising pattern is extremely common in English (far more common, in fact, than the fall–rise variant of the rising pattern), and is found very frequently in non-final intonation groups, where another intonation group follows. But it is very important to note that *an analogous pattern does not occur in German. German possesses, as we have seen, a form which is comparable with the falling–rising variant of the rising pattern, but has no equivalent of the English rise–fall–rise. Because of the high frequency of occurrence of this English form, English-speakers must often make a conscious effort to suppress it when speaking German.*

The difficulties are made more acute by certain superficial affinities between the English rise–fall–rise and the German fall–rise which are not shared by the English falling–rising form. As we have seen, one difference between the two English forms is the presence in the rise–fall–rise of a rising or level phase before the fall; but, as noted above, the German fall–rise, unlike its English counterpart, generally has a level nuclear syllable before the fall, so that in this respect the forms are similar. The main differences between the German form and the English rise–fall–rise pattern are thus the overall higher pitch and the steeper and more sudden pitch movements in the former. It is important to distinguish these forms because the German fall–rise has very different functions from the English rising–falling–rising pattern.

English has a further pattern which has no direct counterpart in German but again has a superficial resemblance to another form, in

this case the narrow variant of the rise. This English pattern may be called the low rise, *as its main characteristic is that the pitch remains fairly low throughout, rising only slightly at the end:*

I **think** so   we can **try**

This form is quite similar to the narrow variant of the rise, but differs from it in its overall pitch level, which is noticeably lower. Indeed, it often becomes so low as to produce a 'creaky' voice quality. Such a form does not, however, exist in German, *where all rises end relatively high within the speaker's range.*

VARIANTS OF THE LEVEL PATTERN

Variants of the level pattern differ primarily in the *height* of the level pitch. This forms a continuous scale, the 'weaker' variants being at about the middle of the speaker's range, and the 'stronger' forms being higher. In all cases the characteristic jump up is present, and with the 'strong' forms in particular there may be a brief but audible upward glide at the beginning of the nuclear syllable. Whatever the height of the nucleus, the tail continues its pitch level until the end of the intonation group:

high: ja**wohl**!   guten **Tag**, Herr Müller!

mid: ja**wohl**!   guten **Tag**, Herr Müller!

The level pattern is rather infrequent in English, but it is also subject to a range of variation of a similar kind:

high: **fine**!   I'm **com**ing

mid: **fine**!   I'm **com**ing

NOTATION

A notation system for recording the various nuclear patterns was introduced in the preceding chapter. For the most part, it will not be found necessary to go beyond this to indicate which particular variant is intended. The mark `, for example, can stand for any form of the falling pattern, and the mark ´ for any form of the rise, including the fall-rise. Nevertheless it is sometimes convenient to indicate that a particularly 'weak' or 'strong' form of a nuclear pattern is used, and in this case we need a notation system which allows us to make the necessary distinctions between variants of the same pattern. The following marks may be used for this purpose:

Falling

basic	`	`heute
high	```	``heute
low	ˎ	ˏheute

Rising-falling

basic	ˆ	ˆheute
wide	˜	˜heute
narrow	ˬ	-heute

Rising

basic (wide)	´	´heute
fall-rise	ˇ	ˇheute
narrow	ˏ	ˏheute

Level

| basic (mid) | ‾ | ‾heute |
| high | = | =heute |

5
Heads

We saw in chapter 2 that the intonation group may consist of three parts: head, nucleus, and tail. Of these the nucleus is the most important, since it must always be present, while the head and the tail are optional. We have so far considered the pitch pattern of the nucleus and tail, which together form the nuclear pattern. Though the nuclear pattern dominates the intonation group, not only in giving it its most characteristic pitch features but also in determining its basic meaning, the head is also significant. In this chapter we shall consider the major types of head that occur in German.

In the previous chapters we did not take account of the pitch of the head except in those cases where it was relevant for the identification of the nuclear pattern. In a number of instances we noted that specific nuclear patterns may be identified by a jump up or down from the pitch of the head, and that ambiguities may occasionally arise where a nuclear pattern has the same form as a combination of head and nucleus.

We must now consider the pitch pattern of the head in more detail. The head, like the intonation group as a whole, is not an arbitrary collection of falls and rises, but has a certain *structure*, and this structure determines *where* the pitch may fall or rise and how a particular pitch feature is to be interpreted. Consider first the following examples:

(a)

gehen Sie nach **Hau**se!   Bücher sind sehr **teu**er geworden

(b)

ich weiß, daß er **kommt**   warum bist du so **faul**?

(c)

mit dem Geld kann ich nichts **an**fangen

meine Frau hat ein neues **Kleid** gekauft

All these examples have a falling nuclear pattern, and all are preceded by a head. It will be observed that this head has a basically *high* pitch, though in examples of (b) and (c) there are slight exceptions to this: the first syllable of the examples of (b), and the first two syllables of (c), are at a lower pitch.

These deviations are easily explained if we take into account the accentual structure of the intonation group (see p. 7, above). The high pitch of the head does not begin until the *first accented syllable*, and any preceding syllables are pronounced at a lower pitch. These initial unaccented syllables are therefore in a sense separate from the head proper, as they do not share its fundamental pitch characteristic.

Syllables of this kind at the beginning of an intonation group are called the *prehead*. The prehead is of only marginal importance for the meaning, and for most purposes it can be safely ignored. We need only note that it generally has a low to mid pitch. It is possible to have a prehead even if there is no head, if there are unaccented syllables (but no accented ones) before the nucleus, as in the following examples:

ich **weiß**   ist der **Klaus** da?

The head in English intonation groups may also be preceded by a prehead, with exactly the same characteristics as its German counterpart. There is thus no difficulty for the English-speaking learner here.

As we shall see below, the accentual structure is also important for the head in other ways, as in some cases the details of the pattern depend on whether the individual syllables are accented or not.

TYPES OF HEAD

In the examples given so far the head proper (i.e. excluding the prehead) has had a *high-level* pitch. High-pitched heads are in fact the most frequent, and we may regard them as the 'basic' or 'normal' forms. Not all heads are of this type, however. The pitch of the head may differ from the basic high-level form in two main ways: in *height* and in *shape*. Though the pitch of the basic form is high, it is possible to have heads pitched at any height on the continuous scale from high to low. In practice, however, it is convenient to make a simple distinction between a *high* head and a *low* head, though it must be borne in mind that this distinction is not absolute, and that intermediate forms may be found.

As far as the shape is concerned, we have noted that the basic head is level. In fact, as we shall see shortly, the pitch is often not quite static, but the auditory effect is certainly of an approximately level pitch throughout. It is possible, however, to have heads in which the pitch changes in the course of the pattern, the main form that we need to recognize having a *rising* pitch, or rather a series of rises, as discussed below.

The three types of head that we shall consider here are thus the *high head*, the *low head*, and the *rising head*.

The high head

The high head is the one that has been exemplified above. In its basic form it has a high-level pitch extending throughout:

Despite the overall impression of a steady high-level pitch, this form is not quite as straightforward as would appear from this description. In order to appreciate this, we must put the pitch under the magnifying glass, as it were, so as to show in more detail the small undulations which are important for the distinctive character of this pattern.

When we look at the high head in this way, we find that there are slight rises and falls within the pattern, and that the rises take place *on the accented syllables*. The pattern thus actually has the following shape:

The accented syllables rise slightly, while the unaccented syllables drift downwards back to the original pitch. This movement is often very slight, and in attempting to imitate it one must not exaggerate the rises and falls. But neither can it be ignored completely, as it is characteristic of the high head in German. The general effect of this upward thrust is to give more prominence to the accented syllables than to the unaccented ones.

In addition to this rising and falling movement *within* the head, the *whole head* may drift upwards or downwards, though without departing too much from the overall high-level pitch of the pattern. The general tendency is for the head to drift towards the height of the following nuclear syllable. Where the nucleus begins high, the head may rise towards it, and where it begins low the head may sink downwards, as in the following examples:

wir müssen es bloß ver**such**en

das hat er mir gerade er**zählt**

The same effect may be observed with the rising nuclear pattern:

ist dein Vater nach **Amer**ika gefahren?

Before the *level* nuclear pattern a slight difference is found. Since this nuclear pattern is characterized by a jump up on the nuclear syllable (see p. 19, above), the head often drops quite considerably at the end to allow for the jump:

wenn du morgen früh noch **da** bist . . .

None of these variations is of any real significance for the meaning, and all these forms may be grouped together as variants of the high head.

A high-level pitch is also characteristic of the most frequent head in English. Although it is basically very similar to the German form, its auditory effect is somewhat different, and this difference can be attributed to the slight undulations in the pattern which we have noted above. Whereas the accented syllables of the high head in German have a basically upward *tendency, in the typical English form of the analogous pattern the accented syllables have a slightly* downward *tendency. The unaccented syllables tend to rise rather than fall in order to restore the original pitch. There are thus undulations in the pitch in both languages, but they are like mirror images of each other:*

German:

English:

Again it must be emphasized that these pitch fluctuations are only slight, but they are sufficient to make the two patterns sound noticeably different. The upward tendency of the accented syllables in German gives the pattern a rather more urgent, vigorous impression to the English ear. The English-speaker can obtain the same effect when speaking German by endeavouring to keep the accented syllables at a higher and more level pitch than he is accustomed to.

With the rising-falling-rising nuclear pattern in English, which, as noted above (p. 27), has no counterpart in German, the most commonly-found head has a still more marked falling, or often rising-falling, tendency in the accented syllables:

you can go if you really **want** to

This pattern is characteristically English, and must be avoided in German. The tendency to use such a pattern is particularly strong with the German fall-rise variant of the rising nuclear pattern, which, as we have seen, has some affinity with the English rising-falling-rising pattern.

The variations in the overall shape of the head in German – the drifting upwards or downwards towards the pitch height of the nucleus – are equally applicable to English, and should therefore create no problems for the learner.

The low head

At the other end of the scale from the high head is the *low head*. Here the pitch is kept fairly low and level throughout. This head may again be preceded by a prehead, with a low or mid pitch, so that there may be a jump *down* on the first accented syllable of the intonation group.

das konnt' ich aber gar nicht **wissen**

The low-level character of this pattern prevails throughout accented and unaccented syllables, so that here we do not find the pitch fluctuation which is characteristic of the high head.

There is a tendency for this pattern, too, to drift towards the pitch of the nuclear syllable of the intonation group. Before a high or mid-pitched nucleus the pattern becomes higher, while before a low-pitched nucleus there may even be a drift downwards to a still lower pitch:

When this head occurs before the low variant of the falling pattern (see p. 23, above), which, it will be recalled, jumps down to a low-level pitch, a slight modification takes place. Since the jump down is essential for the low fall, the head preceding it cannot end low. In this case the low head may drift upwards, or the last syllable may be pitched somewhat higher, e.g.

or:

English has a low-pitched head which is entirely analogous to the German form. Since there is little or no difference between the treatment of accented and unaccented syllables in this type of head, the forms found in the two languages are more or less the same. There is also a similar kind of variation in the two languages before different heights of nucleus.

The rising head

The rising head in fact consists of a series of rises, the number depending on how many accented syllables are contained in the head. Each accented syllable is low and level, with the rises taking place on the unaccented syllables, if there are any. In the absence of unaccented syllables between the accented ones, the rise takes place in the accented syllables themselves. Each rising movement is thus analogous to that found in the rising nuclear pattern:

warum ist Hans wieder **weg**gefahren?

The height reached by each of the rises is variable, but it is approximately the same for each rise in the head, e.g.

or:

It can also be seen that this rising movement is quite different from the rise found in accented syllables of the high head. In the rising head the rise is much more marked and deliberate, and takes place primarily in the unaccented syllables; the accented syllables have a *jump down* to the original low pitch.

This head may also have variants determined by the height of the following nucleus, but there is less scope for an upward or downward drift owing to the range of the pattern itself. Before a wide fall, for example, we may find a variant such as the following:

English has a rising head which is similar to the German form, the only difference being a tendency for the accented syllables to have a slightly falling movement which is uncharacteristic of German:

why don't you ask him to go **away**?

It is useful to have some means of indicating which of these heads is employed in a given case, and, as with the nuclear patterns, it is possible to incorporate marks in a printed text. Since the different patterns depend on the presence of at least one accented syllable (in the absence of an accented syllable we have only a 'prehead' at a mid to low pitch, and no head proper) we may conveniently combine the indication of the type of head with accent marks placed before each accented syllable. The accent marks used in the head are all vertical, as follows:

High head   ˈ   ˈheute
Low head   ˌ   ˌheute
Rising head   ‖   ‖heute

6
Further Aspects of the Intonation Group

In the preceding chapters we have considered the various heads and nuclear patterns of German, together with their variants. The basic unit of intonation, however, is neither the head nor the nuclear pattern but the *intonation group* as a whole, and there are a number of characteristics of this unit that need further discussion.

HEADS AND NUCLEAR PATTERNS

The intonation group generally contains both a head and a nuclear pattern. If we take the basic forms of each (four nuclear patterns and three heads) we have twelve possible combinations. Adding the variants, of course, we obtain an indefinite number of possibilities, since the variation is on a continuous scale.

In principle, we may probably say that all twelve of these basic combinations are possible, but in practice some are found only exceptionally. The rising head, in particular, is somewhat restricted. It occurs only rarely with the high-ending patterns, especially the level one, with which it seems to be almost incompatible. When we include the variant forms, we note that there is a tendency for the rising head, which is the 'strongest' of the three, to be combined with 'strong' forms of the nuclear patterns, though this is certainly not an absolute restriction. The same applies to particularly high forms of the high head; these, too, tend to combine with 'stronger' variants of the nuclear patterns.

The most widely used head, which occurs freely with any of the nuclear patterns or variants, is a moderately high form of the high head. Such a form can with some justification be regarded as the 'basic' or 'normal' head, other forms being used only when a special meaning is intended (see chapter 11, below).

PITCH RANGE

In addition to the variants of the individual heads and nuclear patterns, the intonation pattern of the *whole* intonation group is subject to variation and adjustment. Some of these variations arise from the shade of meaning that the speaker wishes to convey, others simply from the context in which the intonation group occurs.

One important kind of variation here is in the *overall pitch range* of the intonation group. We have already observed that speakers may vary among themselves in the pitch range that they use for speech, depending on their sex, age, or other personal characteristics. Such variations are, of course, not under the control of the speaker. They are, at least in the short term, permanent features of individuals and are meaningless from the point of view of intonation except in so far as they communicate information about the identity of the speaker. In a description of the distinctive intonation patterns of the language they must clearly be discounted. In the preceding chapters this has been done by not giving any absolute value to 'high' and 'low' pitch in the descriptions; these are always relative to the speaker's range which is indicated by the upper and lower lines in the examples.

This pitch range is, however, only the *normal* range of the speaker, where 'normal' is to be understood as including the speaker's emotional state, the circumstances under which he is speaking, and so on. Where the speaker's state is not normal, or where the circumstances deviate from the usual conditions of conversational speech, then the speaker may adjust or modify his pitch range. When speaking with special emotional emphasis, or more loudly than usual, the speaker is likely to *extend* his pitch range; a calm or quiet utterance may have *reduced* pitch range.

Variations of this kind do not affect the shape of the patterns as such such but simply their range. With an extended range, falls and rises will have a wider movement, high pitches will be higher and low pitches lower. With a reduced range, pitch movements become smaller and less marked.

The following examples show the effect of these modifications on the pitch patterns:

ich weiß nicht wie er heißt

normal range:

extended range:

reduced range:

weißt du wie er heißt?

normal range:

extended range:

reduced range:

It is easy to see that there may be difficulties here. We have observed that the individual nuclear patterns, and also the rising head, have variants which differ in the range or height of the pitch. What, then, is the difference between this variation and that which affects the intonation group as a whole? In fact, ambiguity may certainly arise here; it might be difficult in a particular case to decide whether the high pitch of an utterance is to be interpreted as belonging to a high variant of a pattern or to a basic form where the overall pitch range has been widened.

In practice, such ambiguity is probably rare, since the two cases can generally be distinguished. The overall widening or narrowing of range not only affects the *whole* intonation group, but is also often accompanied by other differences from normal speech, such as differences of loudness or voice quality, etc. This means that we are generally able to distinguish high or low pitch in an utterance which has normal range from high or low pitch which results from the extension or reduction of the normal range.

PITCH HEIGHT

The pitch of an utterance may be not only extended or reduced, it may also be shifted bodily up or down so that both upper and lower limits of the range are raised or lowered. For example, the utterance *ich `weiß es nicht* could be pronounced at various heights:

high:

mid:

low:

Speakers generally use a higher pitch level when their utterance is intended to attract more attention, especially when they are introducing a new topic in conversation or reading aloud. This can easily be observed by listening to radio news bulletins, since newsreaders regularly shift their whole pitch level upwards when commencing a new item of news, and will gradually lower the pitch level in succeeding intonation groups until the next new item or topic is introduced. Sometimes, too, a particularly tragic or serious item may be introduced at a lower level, or an especially surprising one at an extra high level. But variation such as this is not confined to newsreaders; all speakers are able to manipulate the pitch level in this fashion.

As can be seen from the above example, this kind of variation again does not affect the shape of the pattern itself but simply the absolute value of the top and the bottom of the range of the utterance.

Neither the extensions and reductions of range nor the variations of height discussed here are peculiar to German, but are almost certainly found in all languages. The English learner of German is therefore not likely to misinterpret features such as this in listening to German or to fail to adjust his own speech according to similar principles when speaking German. Though this area of the intonation of the language is difficult to subject to detailed analysis because various kinds of pitch feature are simultaneously present, it should give little or no difficulty to the foreign learner.

7

Intonation Group Sequences

Most of the examples given in the preceding chapters have been of individual utterances consisting of single intonation groups. Many utterances are more complex than this, however, with not just one, but two, three, four, or even more intonation groups, combined together into sequences. Such sequences are not just an arbitrary succession of patterns, but fall into several clearly-defined types according to the patterns they contain.

In this chapter we shall consider the basic kinds of sequences of intonation groups that occur in German. The simplest are, of course, those containing only two intonation groups, and these will serve as our starting-point. Longer sequences can, in fact, be seen as expansions or elaborations of these simple types.

In considering these sequences it is important to keep in mind the fundamental distinction between the two kinds of nuclear pattern described in chapter 3: the low-ending and the high-ending patterns. This distinction is crucial for an understanding of the different kinds of sequences and of the function of the individual intonation groups within the sequence.

SEQUENCES OF TWO INTONATION GROUPS

There are four possible combinations of the two basic types of patterns in sequences of two intonation groups: high-ending + low-ending, low-ending + low-ending, low-ending + high-ending, and high-ending + high-ending. All these occur in German, and they all have rather different characteristics, as discussed below. The use of different types of sequence is significant for the meaning of the utterance, as will be seen in chapter 13, below.

High-ending + low-ending sequence

The most common and most important sequence of two intonation groups has a high-ending pattern in the first intonation group and a low-ending pattern in the second. The former may be rising or level, and the latter either falling or rising-falling. The following are examples of such sequences (/ indicates the division between the intonation groups):

wenn das Wetter so ˉbleibt / hat der Ausflug keinen ˋSinn
ich weiß ˉwirklich nicht / ob es sich ˆlohnt
geheime ´Sorgen / sind eine schwere ˋLast
ich kann mir ´denken / daß es sehr ˆschwer ist

(These combinations of patterns are assigned to these examples merely for illustration; in principle *all* these examples could be said with *all* these sequences of patterns. The use of these different high-ending and low-ending patterns is, of course, significant for the meaning, as discussed in chapter 14 below.)

The nuclear patterns given here also include the variants discussed in chapter 4. Thus the fall may be high, mid, or low, and the rise may be a fall-rise, or a narrow rise, and so on. The third example, therefore, could equally well be:

geheime ˇSorgen / sind eine schwere ˮLast
or
geheime ´Sorgen / sind eine schwere ˎLast

In English the basic kind of sequence also has a high-ending pattern followed by a low-ending pattern, but since the range of patterns occurring in the two languages is not identical, there are different possibilities here. It will be recalled that the same two basic low-ending patterns – the fall and the rise-fall – can be found in both languages, but English has two additional types in the high-ending category which have no equivalent in German: the rising-falling-rising and the low-rising patterns. Both these additional forms are, in fact, quite common in English in non-final intonation groups, as in the type of sequence under discussion here, alongside the high-rising and level patterns, and it is especially in such cases, therefore, that the English-speaker is tempted to use them. The English learner must make a special effort to avoid his low-rising and rising-falling-rising patterns, and instead to use either the (high) rise or the level pattern. The level pattern is not at all frequent in English, but is extremely common in German in non-final intonation groups, and its use must therefore be cultivated by the English learner.

We have already noted (in chapter 4, above) that the fall–rise variant of the rising nuclear pattern in German is deceptively similar to the English rising–falling–rising pattern. Since both of these occur readily in non-final intonation groups before a final low-ending pattern, the English-speaker is particularly likely to equate the two in this position. The differences in the forms of the patterns must be borne in mind, however. The English rising–falling–rising form will really not do as a substitute for the German fall–rise.

Low-ending + low-ending sequence

This type of sequence has a low-ending pattern in *both* intonation groups. Either the falling or the rising-falling pattern may occur in either intonation group, though there is a tendency for the same pattern to be repeated, i.e. for fall to be followed by fall, and rise–fall to be followed by rise–fall. This is only a tendency, however, and not an absolute rule. Examples are:

> wo ist denn ˋMax / dein ˋBruder?
> diese ˆAussicht / ist ˆherrlich

A similar type of combination occurs in English with the equivalent patterns.

Low-ending + high-ending sequence

A sequence with a low-ending pattern followed by a high-ending pattern is rather restricted, occurring primarily in utterances containing so-called 'tag questions' (e.g. *nicht wahr*, *oder*, etc. attached to the end). The final high-ending pattern is always rising, not level:

> Sie ˋkennen sich schon / ´oder?
> er fährt doch ˆmit / ´nicht wahr?

Where the first intonation group in this type of sequence has a fall, the pattern of the whole becomes rather similar to the falling–rising variant of the rising nuclear pattern. Thus the following two utterances, which are clearly very different in meaning, may be superficially rather similar in form:

> er ˋkommt / ´nicht?
> er ˇkommt nicht

In both cases there is a fall on *kommt* and a rise on *nicht*, but the first consists of two intonation groups forming a sequence and the second is a single intonation group. In the first, therefore, there are two nuclei with two independent patterns, while the fall and the rise are two halves of one pattern in the second. In most cases there will be differences of rhythm and of prominence of the individual syllables which will serve to indicate which version is intended, but occasionally the forms may be identical and ambiguity may result. Here, the context may be required to suggest the appropriate interpretation.

English has forms which are exactly parallel to these German sequences:

> it's ˋraining / ´isn't it?
> you ˆknow / ´do you?

Some words of caution must be expressed here, again with regard to the low-rising and rising-falling-rising patterns. A very common sequence of intonation groups in English has a falling (or rising-falling) pattern in the first intonation group, and a low-rising *pattern in the second. Examples are (where ⸜indicates the low rising nuclear pattern):*

> you can ˋask him / if you ⸜like
> it'll be ˋfinished / to ⸜morrow

This sequence is extremely frequent in English, and it has an important function in the language (see chapter 13, below). But it does not occur in German *and must therefore be specifically avoided.*

Another pattern which is possible after a fall in English is the rise-fall-rise, e.g. (˜ indicates this pattern):

> you can take the ˋbus / if you ˜want to

Again this is lacking in German.

These last two cases, where a low-ending pattern is followed by a high-ending pattern other than the high rise, create special difficulties for the English learner of German. Though the learner must suppress these sequences when speaking German, they are so common in English, and are so bound up with the whole structure of English sentences, that the learner finds it difficult to find suitable alternative intonation patterns. As we shall see in chapter 13, producing German equivalents of such sequences may involve changing the structure of the sentence.

High-ending + high-ending sequence

Sequences of intonation groups with a high-ending pattern in each are also possible, but not very frequent. The level pattern is again excluded from occurrence in the second intonation group, so that here the second pattern is always a rise. In fact, the level pattern is also very uncommon in the first intonation group when a rise follows in the second, so that for the most part this type of sequence consists of rise + rise (though the rise may be any of the variants, including the fall-rise). Examples are:

> wenn es Sie nicht ´stört / darf ich eine ´Frage stellen?
> ist das Herr ˇMüller / der Di´rektor?

This type of sequence is also found in English, again with restrictions on the level pattern, and with the qualification that the high-ending patterns also include the low rise and the rise–fall–rise, as well as the high rise.

LONGER SEQUENCES

The sequences we have considered so far have contained only two intonation groups. Longer, often much longer, sequences are also encountered, especially in more formal styles of speech, in reading aloud from a written text, and so on. The intonation patterns occurring in these longer sequences are basically analogous to the types so far considered, and can be seen as extensions or elaborations of them.

Extensions of high + low sequences

The most usual way of extending this type of sequence is to use a high-ending pattern in *all* the non-final intonation groups. The same high-ending pattern is often found in all these intonation groups, but this is by no means always the case. Examples are:

> wenn es viel ‾Schnee gibt / sind alle ‾Zugangsstraßen / nicht be
>   `fahrbar
> bevor ich unter´schreibe / muß ich mich über´zeugen / daß
>   alles `stimmt

It is also possible to have more than one low-ending pattern at the end of the sequence:

als ich in der ´Schweiz war / hab' ich `Max / deinen `Bruder
  gesehen

And in still longer sequences both the non-final high-ending and the
final low-ending pattern may be repeated:

letzte ´Woche / wie ich in ¯London war / hat es ge`froren / und
  ge`schneit

Extensions of low + low sequence

The sequence of low-ending patterns may be extended indefinitely:

wo ist denn `Max / dein `Bruder / und seine `Frau?
er hat mir doch erˆzählt / daß er morgen ˆfrüh / schon `wieder
  hingeht

Extension of low + high sequence

With the low + high sequence, the non-final low-ending pattern may be
repeated:

das ist `Max / dein `Bruder / ´nicht wahr?

Or it may be preceded by a high-ending pattern:

bis zu den ´Alpen / kann man doch nicht ˆsehen / ´oder?

More than one final rising pattern in such sequences is, however,
unusual.

Extensions of high + high sequence

The sequence of high-ending patterns may be repeated indefinitely:

im ´Sommer / wenn es ´heiß ist / gehst du oft ´schwimmen?

All these types of sequence may be further extended by the addition
of still more intonation groups, though short sequences are more common in ordinary conversation. Some of these longer sequences may
introduce further complexities, and these will be taken up later in
chapter 13.

*In English, the basic types of sequence may be extended in exactly
the same way. Here are some examples:*

last ˜week / when I was in ˜London / I met `John / your `friend
when you've done ˜that one / you'll have `finished / ´won't you?

*The sequences with a final low rise or rise–fall–rise, which do not
occur in German, may be similarly extended by the addition of further
low-rising or rising-falling-rising patterns:*

I shall be in `Scotland / for ˯Christmas / I ex ˯pect
we can go for a `picnic / on ˜Wednesday / if it's ˜fine

8

The Role of the Nucleus

So far we have been concerned with the various intonation patterns found in German and with their structure. Reference to the meaning or function of intonation has been kept to a minimum in order not to distract attention from the pitch patterns themselves. It is with the various aspects of this meaning that we shall be concerned in the remaining chapters of this book.

The only part of the intonation group that *must* be present is the nucleus: every intonation group must have a nucleus even if there is no head or tail, and, as we have seen, the place of the nucleus within the intonation group is variable. The first aspect of the meaning of intonation that we shall consider is the role of the nucleus and of its position in the intonation group.

THE MEANING OF THE NUCLEUS

It is important to note that there is no *absolute* restriction on where the nucleus may occur; it can in principle coincide with any word in the intonation group. Thus, in the utterance *mein Vater hat ein neues Auto gekauft*, pronounced with a single intonation group and hence with one nucleus, each of the words could take the nucleus, with a different meaning in each case:

1. **mein** Vater hat ein neues Auto gekauft (nicht *dein* Vater).
2. mein **Va**ter hat ein neues Auto gekauft (nicht mein *Bruder*).
3. mein Vater **hat** ein neues Auto gekauft (ich sagte, er *hat* eins gekauft, nicht daß er eins kaufen *wird*).
4. mein Vater hat **ein** neues Auto gekauft (nicht *zwei*).
5. mein Vater hat ein **neu**es Auto gekauft (kein *altes*).
6. mein Vater hat ein neues **Au**to gekauft (kein *Fahrrad*).
7. mein Vater hat ein neues Auto ge**kauft** (nicht *gemietet*).

We could pronounce all these versions of this utterance with the same intonation pattern (for example, a falling nuclear pattern preceded by a high head), but with variations depending simply on the position of the nucleus in the intonation group. (1) and (2) would have no head, and (7) no tail, and the others would differ merely in the length of the head and tail.

As far as the meaning is concerned, it is clear from the additions given in brackets in each case (these are simply suggestions and other interpretations would be possible) that the position of the nucleus depends on the item in the utterance that is being singled out as the main piece of 'news', so to speak, the word that is being contrasted with other possibilities. The contrast does not need to be quite as explicit as that suggested by the meaning given here. In (2), for instance, *Vater* does not have to be expressly contrasted with some other word such as *Bruder* or *Sohn*; the sentence may be said as a response to another utterance such as *Hans hat ein neues Auto gekauft* or indeed simply as a reply to the question *wer hat ein neues Auto gekauft?* Similarly, version (6) does not necessarily imply a contrast between *Auto* and some other word; it may be an answer to *was gibt's Neues?* or may indeed presuppose no previous utterance at all.

In other words, therefore, the nucleus does not indicate contrast as such but simply serves to identify the main 'point' of the utterance, the principal piece of information as opposed to what is subordinate, has already been mentioned, or is assumed to be already known to the listener. The 'same' utterance can be said in such a way as to make a variety of different 'points', as the above examples show. The basic content in all cases is the same, but by varying the position of the nucleus the utterance can be made to have quite different communicative significance.

THE PLACE OF THE NUCLEUS

The kind of meaning that the nucleus has is evidently such that it will not generally be possible to predict with certainty where it will occur within an intonation group. What the main communicative point of an utterance is will clearly depend on the context in which the utterance is used, on what has been said before, and the particular communicative effect intended by the speaker, and all these are not usually predictable from the utterance itself. Nevertheless, it is possible to go a little further than this, since what the speaker wishes to communicate and the context in which he says it are also reflected in other features of utterances besides the intonation. It is therefore often possible to relate, in however inconsistent and unreliable a fashion, the place of the nucleus to these other features. The aspects of an utterance that are relevant here are (a) what is 'new' and what is 'given', (b) the order of words in the utterance, and (c) the type of word involved. The interplay of these various features with the position of the nucleus is complex and variable, and though it is not possible to give precise rules for their relationships, a discussion of the factors involved will serve to clarify the significance of the nucleus and its position.

In fact, despite the complexity of this area of the language, placement of the nucleus within the intonation group does not seem to be a serious problem for English-speakers learning German, which is a good indication that the principles involved are the same in both languages. Syntactic differences between the two languages, in particular the different position of the verb, do lead to differences in the application of these principles, however, and it is worth while attempting to understand the details, even if they rarely create problems for the learner.

'NEW' AND 'GIVEN'

We have seen that the nucleus occurs on an item of 'news', on a part of the utterance that is being presented by the speaker as something that the hearer is not expected to know already. We may make a distinction between those parts of the utterance that are *new* in this sense and those that are *given*, i.e. which are, or are assumed by the speaker to be, common knowledge for both speaker and hearer, either because they have been mentioned before, or because they are implicit in the context of the utterance, or even because they are assumed background knowledge. Examining the above examples once more, we see that their different meanings arise from what they convey as 'new' and what they take to be 'given'.

Example (2), with the nucleus on *Vater*, would only really make sense if there had already been mention of *ein neues Auto kaufen*, i.e. if this part of the utterance were 'given'. Example (6), on the other hand, with the nucleus on *Auto*, is rather wider in its range of suitable contexts. There need be nothing 'given' here at all (as in the cases mentioned above where this would be a response to *was gibt's Neues?*). or, at the other extreme, everything except *Auto* could be 'given' (if, for example, this were a contradiction of *dein Vater hat ein neues Fahrrad gekauft*).

There is therefore a relationship between the location of the nucleus within the intonation group and the 'newness' or 'givenness' of various parts of the utterance. As a general rule (though subject to an exception to be mentioned shortly) we may say that, though 'new' and 'given' items may occur anywhere in the utterance, *the nucleus will always coincide with the last new item in the intonation group*. It follows from this that anything which occurs *after* the nucleus must always be 'given', while anything occurring *before* the nucleus may be either 'new' or 'given'. This accounts for the rather limited number of appropriate contexts for the first examples given above, where the nucleus is at the beginning of the intonation group, and the wider range of contexts for the later examples, where the nucleus is towards the end. An *early* nucleus effectively makes almost all the intonation group 'given', while a *late* nucleus allows it to contain either 'new' or 'given' items.

No intonation group may consist entirely of 'given' items, since there must always be a nucleus, and this must occur on a 'new' item. (An utterance in which everything is already known would also be rather superfluous from a communicative point of view!) Likewise, intonation groups consisting only of 'new' items, though possible, are not frequent, as there are almost always assumptions or suppositions common to both speaker and hearer. Apart from utterances said in complete isolation from *any* context (such as the examples in this book), the nearest we are likely to come to a completely 'new' utterance is at the beginning of a conversation with people we have not met before, but even here there are shared assumptions without which communication could hardly take place.

WORD ORDER

The fact that the nucleus coincides with the last 'new' item in the intonation group, and that consequently anything occurring after the nucleus must be 'given', has important consequences for the order of words in an utterance. Taking the same utterance as an example once more, we see that it is possible to vary the word order. Instead of *mein Vater hat ein neues Auto gekauft* we could also say *ein neues Auto hat mein Vater gekauft*. But because the nucleus must occur on the last 'new' item there are restrictions on the use of this variant. With versions (4), (5), and (6), where the nucleus is on part of the phrase *ein neues Auto*, putting this phrase first is only possible if *mein Vater* is 'given'. Version (6), for example, does not specify whether *mein Vater* is 'new' or not, but if modified so as to put *ein neues Auto* at the beginning then *mein Vater* cannot be 'new':

ein neues **Au**to hat mein Vater gekauft

Similar principles apply with the other versions.

It can be seen, therefore, that producing an appropriate version of an utterance in a particular context is not just a matter of knowing where to put the nucleus. It also involves organizing the items in such a way as to ensure that no 'new' item is placed after the nucleus of the intonation group. In many cases this will mean that the nucleus will tend to occur towards the end of the intonation group, as in the majority of examples given so far.

WORD TYPE

Not all types of words are equally likely to take the nucleus. This again is bound up with the distinction between 'new' and 'given', since some words are usually 'given' rather than 'new'. We may distinguish *lexical* (or 'content') words from *grammatical* (or 'form') words, where the former includes nouns, verbs (except auxiliaries), adjectives, and some adverbs, and the latter includes words such as articles, prepositions, conjunctions, pronouns, auxiliary verbs, some weak adverbs, and particles of various sorts. As a general rule, lexical words tend to be 'new' because of their intrinsically greater content, and grammatical words tend to be 'given' because they rarely constitute the main communicative part of an utterance. Some grammatical words, in particular pronouns, are often quite explicitly 'given' in that they refer back to some other word – generally a noun – that has already appeared in the conversation. (*Er*, for example, refers back to some previously mentioned masculine noun.)

Since grammatical words are usually 'given' they do not normally take the nucleus. This is, however, by no means an absolute rule, and it is perfectly possible for such a word to constitute the nucleus of the intonation group. In the examples given earlier, the nucleus occurs on a grammatical word in versions (1), (3), and (4), and these utterances are in no way deviant or unusual. When the nucleus is on a grammatical word, however, this implies a clear contrast with some other word of the same grammatical type. *Mein* is contrasted with *dein*, *sein*, etc., and *ein* with *zwei*, *drei*, etc.

Similarly, as we have seen above, lexical words are not necessarily 'new', but in specific contexts they may be 'given', according to what has been mentioned before or what is assumed to be known. The relationship between lexical and grammatical words on the one hand, and 'new' and 'given' on the other, is thus one of *likely*, rather than *necessary*, correspondence.

THE 'NORMAL' POSITION OF THE NUCLEUS

On the basis of the above observations it would be possible to regard one particular position of the nucleus in a specific utterance as 'normal' and the rest as in some way 'special'. If we consider that lexical words are generally 'new' and grammatical words generally 'given', and bear in mind that the nucleus will coincide with the last 'new' item in the intonation group, then we could formulate a simple rule for the position of the nucleus in 'normal' cases: *the nucleus will occur on the last lexical word in the intonation group*. The versions of the following utterances given here (the nucleus is in bold type) could thus be regarded as 'normal' in this sense:

1. mein Bruder fährt morgen nach **Lon**don
2. ich gebe meinem Freund ein **Buch**
3. ich gebe ihm ein **Buch**
4. ich gebe es meinem **Freund**
5. ich **ge**be es ihm
6. Werther liebt **Lot**te
7. Werther **liebt** sie
8. Er liebt **Lot**te
9. Er **liebt** sie
10. ich **weiß** es nicht
11. **ken**nen Sie sich schon?

In examples (1), (2), (3), (4), (6), and (8) the nucleus occurs on the final word in the intonation group, since this is lexical, but in (5), (7), (9), (10), and (11) the final word is grammatical and the nucleus must therefore occur on an earlier word, which in (7) and (9) is in penultimate position but in (5), (10), and (11) is still earlier. It will also be noted that in examples (3) and (4), where one object is lexical and the other grammatical, German syntax requires the grammatical item to precede the lexical, thus ensuring that the 'normal' position of the nucleus will be final in both cases.

Such a notion of the 'normal' position of the nucleus is quite useful for utterances which are said in isolation, since in these cases the lexical words will naturally all be 'new' and the context will not provide a contrast which will allow grammatical words to be other than 'given'. But it breaks down when the utterances are put into a specific context which may produce cases of 'given' lexical words and 'new' grammatical words. Here, the 'normal' position can only serve as a reference point in terms of which 'deviations' can be described, and it has no serious theoretical value.

THE VERB AND THE NUCLEUS

In fact, even the rule given here for 'normal' utterances must be modified to accommodate certain cases, including the example discussed earlier, *mein Vater hat ein neues Auto gekauft*. If spoken in isolation, this utterance would have the nucleus on *Auto*, not *gekauft*, even though the latter, as a verb, is the final lexical word in the intonation group. In fact, the rule must be restricted so as to exclude verbs from the category of lexical words: in placing the nucleus in 'normal' cases, verbs are generally treated as grammatical rather than lexical. Here are some examples:

> er hat sein ganzes **Geld** verloren
> weißt du etwa, ob er das **Haus** gekauft hat?
> er ist sicher nach **Haus**e gefahren
> vergiß nicht, deinen **Man**tel mitzunehmen!
> der Dieb hat meine silbernen **Ohr**ringe mitgenommen

As can be seen, in all these 'normal' versions the nucleus occurs not on the verb (which is strictly speaking the last lexical word) but on the preceding lexical word. Why this should be, why verbs should be excluded in this way, is not certain.

The restriction applies equally well to the (normally stressed) prefixes of separable verbs:

> er gibt dreimal im Jahr das **Rauch**en auf
> Otto bringt ihr rote **Ro**sen mit

The position of the verb in the sentence is, of course, one of the major syntactic differences between English and German. Thus, the English equivalent of 'mein Vater hat ein neues Auto gekauft' would be 'my father has bought a new car', where the verb is no longer in final position. If we attempt to obtain an English version which is communicatively equivalent to the German utterance with the nucleus on 'Auto' (the 'normal' version), we find that this involves putting the nucleus on 'car', though it is now in final position. The reverse situation occurs with the nucleus on 'gekauft' in the German utterance: the equivalent English version has the nucleus on 'bought' even though it is not in final position. Thus, the nucleus occurs on the same item in equivalent versions in the two languages, irrespective of its position in the utterance. *The difference between the two languages here is thus purely syntactic, and has nothing to do with intonation except in so far as it affects the position in the intonation group of the item taking the nucleus.*

Of course, it is not always possible to identify the 'same' item in the two languages, as utterances in different languages do not necessarily correspond word for word. Hence this general principle cannot always be applied. As a simple example consider the case where German has a phrase corresponding to a single English word, such as 'Gesellschaft leisten' (accompany), or 'Auto fahren' (drive). For the English utterances:

> can you **drive**?
> she ac**com**panied him

we have the German equivalents

> kannst du **Au**to fahren?
> sie hat ihm Ge**sell**schaft geleistet

The nucleus occurs on equivalent items in the two languages, but whereas in English this item consists of a single word, the verb, which necessarily takes the nucleus, in German it is a phrase, and within the phrase it is the noun, not the verb, which takes the nucleus. But despite the fact that the nucleus occurs on the verb in the English utterance but not in its German equivalent, this is not an exception to the general principle, since it is the whole phrase in the German utterance, and not just the verb, that corresponds to the English verb. If we were to expand the verb in the English version into a phrase, it would follow the same pattern as the German utterances with the corresponding meaning, and have the nucleus on the noun:

> can you drive a **car**?
> she kept him **com**pany

But apart from such cases, the position of the nucleus does not seem to create serious difficulties for the learner, as English-speakers speaking German (and, for that matter, German-speakers speaking English) consistently place the nucleus on the communicatively most appropriate item in the majority of cases. This is evidently an area of the language where the speaker's intuitive feeling for the communicative value of the various parts of his utterance leads him to apply the correct principles. Here the foreign learner has nothing to learn.

9

The Meanings of the Nuclear Patterns: the Fall and the Rise

In considering the meanings of the nuclear patterns we embark on one of the most difficult and controversial areas in the whole of intonation studies. The chief problem is that the meanings appear to be so variable, so much tied to a particular utterance used in a specific context, that it is extremely difficult to make generalizations. And where we feel able to make generalizations, the meanings become so vague as to be of little help in determining when the patterns should be used.

We may begin by considering the meanings of the two most important patterns of German, the fall and the rise. Some of the major questions that arise here can be illustrated by the following examples:

1. es hat ihm ge`fallen
2. es hat ihm ge´fallen

These two utterances differ only in their intonation: (1) has a falling nuclear pattern and (2) a rise. What is the difference in meaning between the two?

At first sight the answer seems to be quite easy: (1) is a statement and (2) a question, and since the only difference between them is in the intonation we could conclude that the fall means 'statement' and the rise means 'question'. Consider, however, the following examples:

3. hat es ihm ge`fallen
4. hat es ihm ge´fallen

Again the only difference between these two utterances is in their intonation: (3) has a fall and (4) a rise. But in this case *both* appear to be questions, though with slightly different implications. It is not possible, therefore, simply to equate 'fall' with 'statement' and 'rise' with 'question'.

One way of solving this problem is to take into account the type of sentence in which the intonation pattern occurs. Both (1) and (2) are *declarative* sentences in which the verb is in second position, while (3) and (4) are *interrogative* sentences, with the verb at the beginning. We could therefore suggest that in declarative sentences fall means 'statement' and rise means 'question', but in interrogative sentences both fall and rise mean 'question' but each carries a slightly different implication. (Note that in order to say this we must distinguish types of sentence *structure*, based on syntactic differences, from types of sentence *use*, based on the role of the sentence in connected speech. 'Declarative' and 'interrogative' refer to different types of structure; 'statement' and 'question' to different types of use. This distinction is important because not all declarative sentences are statements, and not all interrogative sentences are questions. Considerable misunderstandings can result if these two aspects are not kept apart.)

What this approach fails to take account of, however, is that there is an element of meaning, attributable to the intonation pattern, that is the same in (1) and (3), and similarly in (2) and (4). In other words, a given pattern does appear to have something consistent in its meaning, whatever type of sentence structure it occurs with.

This suggests, therefore, that 'statement' and 'question', which seemed to be appropriate as the meanings of the fall and the rise in (1) and (2), are not really the meanings of these patterns at all. This is, in fact, evident from example (2), which, though it *may* be interpreted as a question, *need* not be. It could, for example, be a rather lively contradiction of a previous assertion, and even when used as a question it differs from (3) or (4) in being more in the nature of a statement put forward for ratification or denial than a request for information. Furthermore, example (1), which appears to be a statement, *could*, in appropriate circumstances, be construed as a question, though again one seeking confirmation.

The meanings 'statement' and 'question' are thus inappropriate for these two patterns. They are too restricted, and we must find something more general. In the case of the rising pattern this more general meaning appears to be not 'question' as such, but rather an *appeal to the listener*, who is being invited, or challenged, to respond. Such an implication is naturally very appropriate for questions, but it is not incompatible with statements, which can also invite a response from the listener.

The falling pattern is less easy to characterize, since, in comparison with the rise, it has a somewhat negative connotation: the speaker is *not* making an appeal to the listener, who is at most expected to provide an acknowledgement. It makes the utterance self-sufficient, since it is not dependent on the listener's reply. This type of meaning will, for want of a better term, be called *assertion*, though this is not to be understood as being equivalent to 'statement'. Statements are certainly likely to be assertive in this sense, but it is also possible to have assertive questions.

The difference in meaning between (1) and (2), and (3) and (4), can thus be explained in terms of a distinction between the *assertion* of the fall and the *appeal* of the rise. Both (1) and (3), whether interpreted as questions or as statements, are 'assertions', while both (2) and (4) constitute 'appeals' to the listener. (3) could therefore be described as an 'assertion-question' and (4) as an 'appeal-question'.

It must be emphasized that the terms 'appeal' and 'assertion' are used here in a rather special way. There is a sense, of course, in which every utterance is an 'appeal' to a listener, since the listener is expected, at the very least, to take note of what the speaker is saying. Similarly there is an 'assertion' of a sort in every utterance, since the speaker is always communicating something. But these terms are here intended to have a somewhat more specific connotation; 'appeal' does not just mean 'addressing the listener' but rather addressing him in order to elicit a direct response; 'assertion' does not just mean 'communicating something' but rather making an utterance which does not require a direct response.

Other terms could be used to characterize this distinction. We could perhaps describe the meaning of the rise as 'open' and that of the fall as 'closed'; the former is 'open' to a response, the latter not. Though there is something to be said for such very general terms, they are probably too vague to be helpful, and the terms 'appeal' and 'assertion' will be preferred in this book.

'NORMAL' INTONATION PATTERNS

Though it is important to distinguish 'assertions' from 'statements', and 'appeals' from 'questions', it is evident that there is a relationship between them: it is *likely* that the majority of statements will be assertions and that the majority of questions will be appeals to the listener. Thus, though this correspondence is by no means obligatory, it could nevertheless be seen as *normal*. This concept of 'normality' is, like that of the 'normal' position of the nucleus, of limited value, since the 'normal' pattern could be decidedly *abnormal* in certain specific contexts. But we might say that German-speakers would be likely to use the 'normal' pattern for an utterance unless there is some specific reason for them to do otherwise. Whether there is such a reason depends, of course, on the context of the utterance, and what implication the speaker wishes to convey.

The major sentence types that we may recognize are declarative, interrogative, and imperative. For the purposes of intonation it is also useful to subdivide the interrogative into two types: one which contains a question word (*was, wann, wie, wo, warum*, etc.) and which has the verb in the second position, and one which does not contain such a word and which has the verb at the beginning. If we wish to recognize a 'normal' intonation pattern for these types of sentence we may establish the following rule: *the falling nuclear pattern is 'normal' for all sentence types except the interrogative without a question word, where the rising nuclear pattern is 'normal'*. This will be further exemplified below.

Declarative sentences

As we have seen above, the most usual pattern for declarative sentences is the fall. Here are some further examples:

1(a) mein Bruder ist ˋLehrer
2(a) ich war doch nicht ˋda
3(a) er erwartet diese Nachricht schon seit ˋgestern
4(a) der Kaffee ist ˋgut
5(a) ihr habt alle verˋstanden
6(a) dein Mann ist nach Aˋmerika gefahren

All these could be seen as the 'normal' versions in the sense of the most likely or appropriate for this type of sentence. The falling pattern implies an assertion, a fairly neutral communication as opposed to one that requires a response from the listener. Given the actual content of these examples, however, the falling pattern may be more or less likely in individual cases. We may compare these with the 'same' sentences with a rising nuclear pattern:

1(b) mein Bruder ist ´Lehrer
2(b) ich war doch nicht ´da
3(b) er erwartet diese Nachricht schon seit ´gestern
4(b) der Kaffee ist ´gut
5(b) ihr habt alle ver´standen
6(b) dein Mann ist nach A´merika gefahren

The implication in all these cases is the same: the listener is expected to respond in some way. In specific contexts this might be construed as a question, a challenge, a contradiction, etc., but the likely interpretation may also vary according to the content of the utterance itself. Examples (5b) and (6b) are clearly more likely to be used as questions than (1b) or (2b), if only because they already contain the second person forms *ihr* and *dein*, while it would require an unusual context for examples with the first person forms *mein* and *ich* to constitute questions, and they would more plausibly be used with this intonation if they were contradictions or challenging statements. (In fact, for this same reason, it is not necessarily the case that in (5a) and (6a) the 'normal' intonation is the fall.) But this does not mean that the rising pattern has a variety of different meanings – contradiction, challenge, question, etc. – but that its meaning is general enough to allow for all these interpretations.

Interrogative sentences without a question word

The 'normal' pattern here is the rise. Interrogative sentences are generally questions, and hence the 'appeal' connotation of the rise is particularly appropriate. Here are some further examples:

1(a) hast du meine ´Frau gesehen?
2(a) können wir ´anfangen?
3(a) ist das Buch schon ver´griffen?
4(a) bist du ´sicher?

1(b) hast du meine `Frau gesehen?
2(b) können wir `anfangen?
3(b) ist das Buch schon ver`griffen?
4(b) bist du `sicher?

The falling pattern adds an 'assertive' element which again is subject to a variety of interpretations according to the context. It may suggest that the question is more in the nature of a demand or that it is being asked for a second time. But again it must be stressed that these are not the meanings of the fall but simply interpretations or implications derived from the basic assertive meaning in this specific context.

Interrogative sentences with a question word

It is 'normal' for interrogative sentences with a question word to have the falling nuclear pattern. The following are illustrations:

1(a) wo ist mein `Bleistift hingeraten?
2(a) wann kommt der `Zug an?

3(a) was `machst du?
4(a) wo `ist er denn?
5(a) wie `spät ist es?

1(b) wo ist mein ´Bleistift hingeraten?
2(b) wann kommt der ´Zug an?
3(b) was ´machst du?
4(b) wo ´ist er denn?
5(b) wie ´spät ist es?

The falling pattern here gives a fairly neutral implication, while the rise, with its element of 'appeal', may add a note of extra interest, often of friendliness or politeness (it has been called the *Höflichkeitsmelodie* in this type of sentence). But it can also be used when the speaker is simply repeating a question that has been put to him. A particular case where the rising pattern can be seen as the norm is in intonation groups where the nucleus is on the question word itself, as in:

> ´was hat er gesagt?
> ´wie hoch ist dieser Berg?
> mit ´wem fahren Sie?

This kind of question is often used where the speaker has failed to hear or does not understand or believe what he has been told. The question word identifies the information required; the fact that it takes the nucleus indicates that the remainder of the sentence contains 'given' information (cf. chapter 8, above), and the use of the rising pattern suggests that the speaker is appealing for a restatement of the information already provided or implied. A falling pattern here would suggest not that the information given was not heard or believed but rather that it has yet to be supplied.

The interplay between the structure of the sentence (with its question word), the position of the nucleus, and the pattern used, is particularly evident in such cases as this. Compare, for example, the following versions:

1. wie hoch ist dieser `Berg?
2. wie `hoch ist dieser Berg?
3. `wie hoch ist dieser Berg?
4. ´wie hoch ist dieser Berg?

(1) may be seen as the normal way of putting this question if there has been no previous mention of *Berg*; (2) would be the norm if the

mountain had been mentioned but not its height. (3) implies previous mention of its height but with no precise information as to degree or measurement, while (4) suggests that *all* the information has been given, but must be repeated.

Imperative sentences

Like the interrogative without a question word, the German imperative has the verb at the beginning, but, except in the polite form with *Sie*, where it is identical to the interrogative, it differs in not having a subject. The falling pattern can be regarded as 'normal', as in the following examples:

    1(a)   `tu das nicht
    2(a)   steh `auf
    3(a)   bring doch deine `Frau mit
    4(a)   nehmen Sie bitte `Platz
    5(a)   kommen Sie he`rein

    1(b)   ´tu das nicht
    2(b)   steh ´auf
    3(b)   bring doch deine ´Frau mit
    4(b)   nehmen Sie bitte ´Platz
    5(b)   kommen Sie he´rein

With imperative sentences the 'appeal' element of the rise will generally have the effect of turning the command into a request, or adding a note of urgency, encouragement, impatience, etc., according to the context. A peculiarity of the polite (*Sie*) form of the German imperative is that it is in form identical with the interrogative. Since the falling pattern is normally more appropriate for commands, and the rising pattern more appropriate for questions, the pattern used is often a good indication of this type of sentence:

Imperative	*Interrogative*
kommen Sie he`rein!	kommen Sie he´rein?
gehen Sie nach `Hause!	gehen Sie nach ´Hause?
fahren Sie mit der `Bahn!	fahren Sie mit der ´Bahn?

Since, however, both patterns are possible with both types of sentence, these forms are actually ambiguous out of context, and misunderstandings can arise.

'INCOMPLETE SENTENCES'

We have so far considered the use of the falling and rising nuclear patterns in terms of different types of sentences. It must be borne in mind, however, that the unit of intonation is not the sentence as such but the *intonation group*, which may or may not correspond to a sentence in the grammatical sense. Sentences may often be broken up into a number of intonation groups, so that the intonation group corresponds not to a sentence but to a fragment of a sentence, and in this case it naturally becomes difficult to relate the intonation pattern to the 'sentence type' as such. The principles involved in dividing sentences up into more than one intonation group and in assigning an appropriate pattern to the various sentence fragments will be considered in later chapters. But there is also one case where the intonation group does not correspond to a complete sentence that can be discussed at this point: where the utterance does not in fact contain any sentence in the grammatical sense at all, as in so-called 'incomplete sentences'. This is characteristic of many utterances which we produce as greetings, answers, etc.

If the utterance is not a sentence, how do we determine the 'normal' intonation pattern for it? One way of doing this is to relate it to the sentence type to which it would belong if we were to complete it. Thus the following incomplete sentences could be completed along the lines suggested here:

> Rauchen ver`boten (das Rauchen ist verboten)
> guten `Morgen (ich wünsche Ihnen einen guten Morgen)
> `morgen (er kommt morgen)
> ´morgen? (kommt er morgen?)
> aber `wann? (aber wann kommt er?)

How we choose to complete the sentence clearly depends on the context in which the incomplete sentence is uttered, and there is also evidently a considerable amount of arbitrariness in how we expand the phrase. But it will nevertheless be clear that it is possible to regard incomplete sentences as abbreviated versions of full sentences and thus to assign them to a structural type. The 'normal' intonation pattern will then be determined by the factors discussed above. Since, however, the 'normal' intonation pattern is of no real importance, as it involves isolating an utterance from any context, establishing the sentence type is not a serious problem. Thus, it is not necessary to decide if *morgen* is declarative or interrogative, but only if it is an appeal (for example a greeting, question, challenge, etc.) or an assertion (for example, an answer or a contradiction).

The English-speaking learner will have little difficulty with the falling and rising patterns in German, since both these occur in English, and they are used in broadly analogous ways. Thus the fall in English is most frequently found in declarative and imperative sentences and in interrogatives containing a question word, while the rise is typically found in interrogatives without a question word. The same kind of 'assertive' and 'appeal' implications are conveyed by the patterns in both languages.

Though there is no problem with these patterns themselves difficulties may nevertheless arise because of the presence of other patterns in English which have no direct counterpart in German, as discussed in chapter 3, above. The absence of such patterns in German means that German-speakers may use a fall or rise in utterances where the English-speaker would prefer another pattern. This problem will be taken up again in the next chapter.

10
The Meanings of the Nuclear Patterns: Further Forms

The fall and the rise are the most important nuclear patterns of German. As we saw in chapter 3, however, there are others, namely the rising-falling and level patterns. Furthermore, each of these patterns occurs in a variety of different forms, all of which are distinct in meaning. In this chapter we shall consider the meaning of these various patterns.

THE RISING-FALLING PATTERN

We may recall here that German nuclear patterns fall into two types, *low* ending and *high* ending. This distinction is important, not only for the form but also for the meaning, since the patterns of each type have certain characteristics of their meaning in common. Thus, the rising-falling pattern shares with the other low-ending pattern, the fall, its basically *assertive* meaning (in the sense discussed in the previous chapter); it indicates that the utterance is independent, and does not constitute a direct appeal to the listener. For this reason, it is also likely to be found most frequently in the same types of sentence as the fall — declarative and imperative sentences, and interrogatives with a question word. Like the fall, however, it is not bound to occur in such sentences, as the assertive meaning is not incompatible with questions without a question word. Here are some examples.

> *Declarative:*
> ich ˆweiß
> es ˆschneit schon wieder
> das hab' ich ihm doch er ˆklärt!

> *Imperative:*
> ˆkomm doch mal!
> ˆsetzen Sie sich!
> ˆtu das nicht!

> *Interrogative with a question word:*
> was ˆhast du denn?

woher ˆweißt du das?
wer hat Ihnen ˆdiese Information gegeben?

Interrogative without a question word:
ˆkommt er denn überhaupt?
ist es aber ˆwahr, daß er weg will?
können wir nicht ˆfrüher anfangen?

In all these examples the assertive implication is present, but the rise-fall adds an additional connotation which is lacking in the simple falling pattern. This connotation is that of *personal involvement* in what is said, or an *emotional commitment* of some kind, a suggestion that what is said really matters to the speaker. This meaning is such that the rise-fall is frequently found in exclamations, whatever sentence type they belong to (many are 'incomplete sentences'):

O, wie ˆherrlich!
der Blick is ja ˆfabelhaft
ˆdu bist aber blöd!

It should be noted, however, that the commitment does not need to be genuine or sincere; we frequently find the rise-fall occurring in sarcastic utterances:

das war sehr ge ˆscheit von dir!
bei so einem Regen wäre ein Spaziergang natürlich ˆwunderbar!

In general, the use of this pattern presents no serious difficulties for English-speakers, as the meaning of the English rise-fall is entirely analogous to that of the German form.

THE LEVEL PATTERN

The most characteristic use of the level pattern in German is in non-final intonation groups, i.e. where another intonation group follows (see chapter 7, above, and chapter 13, below). It occurs only rarely independently, being found occasionally in short utterances such as greetings, words of thanks and encouragement, etc. Examples are:

guten ⁻Morgen
⁻schön!
ja⁻wohl!

The implication conveyed by this pattern is of a generally cheerful, unassertive utterance, which neither commits the speaker to anything nor expects a response from the hearer. The pattern is thus most appropriate for ritual expressions such as greetings, which contain little or no information. To use such an intonation pattern with a more weighty or significant utterance would imply that the speaker is treating it as trivial and relatively contentless, as in the following example:

er kommt ‾morgen

Such an intonation pattern with this utterance might suggest that the speaker is bored with, or tired of, the information contained in it, or simply that he takes it to be so self-explanatory as to be hardly worth mentioning.

Although a level pattern is occasionally used in English in expressions of a similar kind with a similar meaning, it is probably even rarer than in German. In neither language is it particularly common. This does not apply, however, to the use of the level pattern in non-final intonation groups in German; here it is very frequent (see chapter 14, below).

THE MEANINGS OF THE ENGLISH PATTERNS WHICH DO NOT OCCUR IN GERMAN

It can be seen that the intonation patterns of German present no real problems of meaning for the English learner, since all occur in English with approximately similar functions, and in the same types of sentences. (There are potential difficulties with the forms of these patterns, of course, as discussed earlier.) This does not mean, however, that the English learner may simply use his English intonation patterns in speaking German, since, as we have seen, an important difference between the two languages is the presence in English of other patterns which German lacks. Learners are thus faced with the problem not of learning to use new and unfamiliar patterns, but rather of learning not to use patterns which to them are usual and natural. In such cases they must learn to replace their English patterns with one of those found in German. This is not altogether easy, as the patterns they must use will for them not be exactly identical in meaning with the English pattern that they would use in the same circumstances. The two English patterns that fall under this heading are the low rise and rise–fall–rise.

The low rise

The English low rise is essentially a non-assertive *pattern; it is frequently used to 'soften' an utterance so as to avoid the matter-of-fact tone of the fall, or the sometimes too aggressive tone of the high rise. Examples are (ˌˌ indicates the low rise):*

> I ˌthink so
> you can if you ˌlike
> it's ˌpossible I suppose
> come a ˌlong
> don't be ˌlate

This non-assertiveness can, according to the context, be interpreted as a lack of commitment or interest ('It doesn't matter to me'), or as warmth and encouragement ('Everything will be all right'). Where such implications are to be conveyed, the falling pattern sounds too curt, while the high rise, with its directness of appeal to the listener, may often sound too strong or aggressive.

The lack of a comparable pattern to the English low rise may well be one of the features that make German sound somewhat formal, indeed slightly abrupt and arrogant, to English ears. The formality and arrogance are, of course, only apparent, and Germans have other ways of softening their utterances (see chapter 15, below). But for English-speakers the difficulty is that they must learn to do without the low rise and instead use patterns which to them are too 'strong', too lacking in informality and warmth. For the most part, the low rise will need to be replaced by the falling pattern in German, together with some suitable 'softening' addition (see chapter 15).

The rise–fall–rise

Nothing is more English than the rise–fall–rise. It is often used instead of the falling pattern in utterances which express some kind of reservation, condition, or concession. Examples are:

> I ˜haven't
> it's ˜true
> they ˜sometimes do

Again, the English-speaker must learn to do without this very frequent pattern when speaking German. Though there is a superficially similar form in German, as discussed on page 27, its function is quite different.

*In non-final intonation groups the difference is less marked (see chapter
14, below), but even here the patterns are not really equivalent.*

THE MEANINGS OF THE VARIANTS OF THE PATTERNS

We noted in chapter 3 that all the nuclear patterns of German are susceptible to a range of variation, principally affecting the pitch range,
but also in some cases the shape of the pattern. Thus the fall may differ
in the height of its starting-point, the level pattern in the height to
which it jumps up; the rise–fall may have an extended range, and the
rise may have an additional falling phase before the start of the rise.

These variations are of significance for the meaning of the patterns,
but the differences of meaning between the variants of one pattern are
of a rather different kind from the differences between the basic patterns themselves. In fact, the meanings of the patterns given so far in
this and the previous chapter apply to *all* the variants; the same basic
connotation of 'assertion' can be associated with the high, mid, or low
variants of the fall, and the same element of 'appeal' is common to all
the variants of the rise, and so on.

The variants of each pattern differ from one another essentially
in what might be called their 'strength', though the term 'strength'
clearly needs further elaboration. In effect, the 'stronger' forms serve
to draw more attention to the nucleus of the intonation group by
making it stand out as a more prominent part of the utterance. Since
the role of the nucleus is, as we have seen, to indicate a part of the
utterance that is regarded as a 'new' piece of information, the main
'focus' of the 'message', it is clear that giving greater prominence to
the nucleus will suggest greater 'newness', or perhaps an element of
surprise or unexpectedness. Such prominence is often given to the
nucleus when it falls on a new topic of conversation. 'Newness', 'surprise', and 'unexpectedness' are relative matters, and hence the variants
form a scale from 'strongest' to 'weakest'. The 'weak' end of the scale
will have the opposite effect; it will play down the significance of the
nucleus, suggesting something expected, even obvious. Compare, for
example the following:

> ein ˘Hund hat ihn gebissen
> ein ˈHund hat ihn gebissen
> ein ˏHund hat ihn gebissen

(for the notational conventions see page 29).

The version with the basic (mid) fall can be taken as the norm. In the 'wide' version, by making the nucleus more prominent the speaker is giving more significance to the word *Hund*; he is emphasizing its importance in this context as part of his message. The 'narrow' form does the opposite: it reduces the intended significance of this part of the utterances, suggesting perhaps that it deserves little attention, or is not newsworthy.

Exactly the same kind of relationship can be found between the variants of the other nuclear patterns. The 'strong' forms increase the prominence of the nucleus and the 'weak' forms reduce it. In the following case with a rising pattern:

> ist dein ´Bruder schon da?
> ist dein ˇBruder schon da?

the first 'basic' version is normal, but the second draws more attention to *Bruder*, suggesting that this item is particularly significant in this context. This version might thus be used in introducing the topic of *Bruder*, or in contrasting it with some other topic that has been mentioned.

English has similar variants to German, and the basic implication of the different variants is the same: the 'stronger' forms make the nucleus more prominent, and the 'weaker' forms make it less prominent. These adjustments will thus be made automatically by English-speakers when speaking German, and difficulties should not arise. But this does depend on mastery of the particular phonetic characteristics of the German forms. The normal form of the German fall, for example, sounds somewhat 'stronger' than the normal English form, because of its high-level nucleus.

11
The Meanings of the Heads

In chapter 5 three types of head were described: *high*, *low*, and *rising*. The first two of these have a basically *level* pitch throughout, though with minor fluctuations dependent on the stress, and the possibility of a general and gradual drift up or down; they differ from each other in their height. Pitch height is a continuously variable feature, with no fixed points, and hence the distinction between the high and low heads cannot be an absolute one; intermediate pitch levels are also possible. Nevertheless, it is convenient to make a basic division between those heads which have a relatively high pitch and those which are relatively low.

The difference of meaning between these two heads can likewise be seen as forming a scale rather than a choice between two completely separate alternatives. The meaning that can be associated with these heads relates to the *relative importance* of the words contained in the head as contributions to the overall meaning of the utterance: a *high* head suggests importance, and a *low* head lack of importance.

The term 'importance' requires some explanation. We are not concerned here with the intrinsic significance of the words, but rather with their significance in this context, with their *communicative* role. Thus, in the following examples:

(a)   ich 'fahre 'morgen nach Ber`lin
(b)   ich ˌfahre ˌmorgen nach Ber`lin

where (a) has a high head and (b) a low head, the implication of (b) is that *fahre* and *morgen* have a relatively low communicative value, that they are pieces of 'known' or 'expected' information. In (a), however, the high head makes *fahre* and *morgen* more prominent, and presents them as having a higher communicative value. Example (b) might thus be appropriate as a response to a question such as 'wo fährst du morgen hin?', the low head in the reply reflecting the fact that this information is simply a repetition of what is contained in the question, and therefore communicates little. Example (a) might be more appropriate as an answer to a more general question such as *warum kommst du nicht mit ins Theater?*, which does not provide this information.

Naturally, as with other uses of intonation, the high and the low head cannot be predicted mechanically from the presence of 'known' or 'unknown' information. The speaker is free to give whatever importance he thinks fit to the parts of his utterances, though the 'newness' of the information is an important deciding factor. Thus, example (a) is certainly not excluded as a possible answer to *wo fährst du morgen hin?*, nor (b) as a possible answer to *warum kommst du nicht mit ins Theater?*. Furthermore, the fact that pitch height is a *scale*, with intermediate points between high and low, means that the speaker is able to adjust the height of the head according to the *relative* importance that he wishes to give to the words contained in the head.

The following are further examples of a similar kind to the above, where the choice of a high or low form may reflect the relative importance of the information in the context in question:

> 'haben Sie den 'neuen Ro'man von ´Grass gelesen?
> ₁haben Sie den ₁neuen Ro₁man von ´Grass gelesen?
> wa'rum 'bringst du deinen `Hund nicht mit?
> wa₁rum ₁bringst du deinen `Hund nicht mit?
> 'fragen Sie 'bitte den `Arzt.
> ₁fragen Sie ₁bitte den `Arzt.

These examples constitute different sentence types, syntactically speaking, from the previous case, but the effect of choosing either the high or the low head is the same: the high head indicates relative importance in the context in question, and the low head indicates relative *lack* of importance, where 'importance' refers to the communicative role of the items in question. In the first pair, the version with the low head might be appropriately used where the topic of reading novels had already been introduced, while the version with the high head suggests no such prerequisite. Similar considerations apply with the other pairs. It must be stated again, however, that the versions with the low head are not obligatory where the items in question have already been mentioned, nor are the versions with the high head obligatory where they have *not* been mentioned.

With the falling nuclear pattern in particular, the effect of using a low head will be to make the pitch of the nucleus stand out, since there will be a jump up to the high or mid-pitch of the nuclear syllable. The extra prominence given to the nucleus also applies to the meaning:

by reducing the significance of everything that precedes the nucleus, the nucleus itself, as the only piece of significant information in the intonation group, is thrown into relief.

The third type of head, the *rising* head, is somewhat different in character from either of the other two forms. This type, with its strong pitch movement, is very emphatic, and hence it gives, like the high head, considerable significance to the items contained in the head, but the effect is very different from that of the high head. The rising head in fact adds a special connotation, which might be called *force*. This forcefulness might, according to context, be interpreted as urgency, impatience, excitement, etc., as appropriate. The following are typical examples where such an intonation might be used:

> ich ‖kann es ‖einfach nicht ˋschaffen!
> wa‖rum sagst du ‖endlich nicht ˋnein?
> ver‖lang ‖doch dein ˋGeld zurück!

Provided that the phonetic forms of these heads have been mastered (see chapter 5, above) the appropriate use of the high, low, and rising heads should not present a problem to the English-speaker, since analogous forms occur in English, with similar functions. The following examples will illustrate their use in English.

> ˈwhere've you ˈput the ˋsalt?
> ˌwhere've you ˌput the ˋsalt?
> ‖ where've you ‖put the ˋsalt?

The first of these might be regarded as the most normal, while the second, which reduces the significance of the first part of the utterance, could be used if, for example, other similar questions had already been asked (where've you put the bread? where've you put the milk? where've you put the sugar?) and the only unknown part of the utterance was the word 'salt'. The third example is a forceful and emphatic enquiry.

12
The Role of the Intonation Group

In considering the meaning of intonation we have so far restricted ourselves to single intonation groups and their component parts. As we saw in chapter 7, however, utterances may be divided up into more than one intonation group. Hence the first question to consider is the nature of the factors which determine how many intonation groups the utterance will contain.

We may begin with a number of examples of utterances pronounced in different ways, with different numbers of intonation groups:

I
- (a) ich fahre morgen nach Ber`lin
- (b) bist du sicher, daß er ´kommt?
- (c) wieviel Geld `brauchst du denn?

II
- (a) ich fahre ´morgen / nach Ber`lin
- (b) bist du ´sicher / daß er ´kommt?
- (c) wieviel ´Geld / `brauchst du denn?

The versions under I consist of a single intonation group, while the 'same' utterances under II consist of two. (The actual patterns given here are simply typical for these types of utterances and are not at issue here; other patterns could be substituted with the same effect.) What is the difference in meaning between the examples of I and the corresponding examples of II?

In terms of their grammatical and lexical (i.e. vocabulary) content the versions with one and two intonation groups are, of course, identical, but there is nevertheless a difference of meaning between the two sets as a result of the different number of intonation groups. With one intonation group the utterances give the impression of being a single entity, *a single piece of information*, while with two intonation groups there appear to be *two pieces of information*. Just what is meant by a 'piece of information' in this case is rather hard to define, but it seems clear that in speaking we – generally quite unconsciously – present what we are saying in sections or 'chunks', where each such section constitutes a single communicative item in some sense. Our utterances thus resemble not so much an unbroken thread of information as a chain consisting of links, each link containing a certain amount of information.

Such a chain-like sequence of units is, of course, found in the grammatical structure of utterances, where we may find sentences, clauses, and phrases as bearers of the grammatical 'information'. But it is evident that the kind of units that we are concerned with in intonation, and which correspond to intonation groups, are not grammatical units as such. As the above examples show, the same grammatical units (the sentences of I and II) may be pronounced in different ways, with different numbers of intonation groups. Division into intonation groups is therefore largely independent of grammatical grouping, and the units produced by this division are not grammatical units as such, but units of 'communication' or of 'information' in a somewhat different sense.

Since we are accustomed to thinking of our utterances as consisting of grammatical units such as sentences it is at first difficult for us to recognize that they also have another kind of structure in which the units are not grammatical but communicative. It will also be evident that such communicative units are likely to be far more elusive and less easily defined than units of grammar, as speakers may vary considerably in what they choose to make into a unit, depending on the circumstances in which the utterance is made, the speed of speech, and so on.

Despite this variability, grammatical structure is not wholly irrelevant for the division of utterances into intonation groups. Grammatical structure, too, is in part a reflection of how a speaker chooses to divide up what he has to say into convenient units, and it is therefore often possible to establish at least certain likely correspondences between specific grammatical structures and particular ways of dividing utterances up into intonation groups. Nevertheless, it must be emphasized that these correspondences are rarely obligatory, and speakers can and do deviate from them very frequently.

In the remainder of this chapter we shall examine some of the chief ways in which the grammatical structure of utterances may determine the likely division into intonation groups.

It may be observed here that the basic principles involved in deter-
mining the number of intonation groups in an utterance are exactly
the same in German and English: division into intonation groups
reflects the number of 'information' units in the utterance. In general
terms, therefore, the discussion that follows of the likely correspon-
dences between specific types of sentence and intonation groups is
equally applicable to English. The English-speaking learner is thus
unlikely to have serious difficulties here. Nevertheless, there are certain
differences of detail arising partly from the differences of grammatical
structure in the two languages and partly from the differences of
intonation structure. These divergences will be taken up below.

THE SIMPLE SENTENCE

As a general rule it may be stated that a simple sentence (i.e. one
consisting of a single clause) will regularly consist of a single intonation
group. This is a fairly natural correspondence which reflects the fact
that a single piece of 'information' (in the sense used earlier) is likely
to constitute a single grammatical unit, too. The following examples
can thus be regarded as normal in this respect:

> es ist schon sieben Uhr `dreißig
> wie ist das `Wetter heute?
> kommst du mit ins The´ater?
> nimm doch einen `anderen!

It is of course possible for these utterances to be divided up into
more than one intonation group if the speaker chooses to make them
particularly 'weighty', though this is more likely with longer clauses.
The third example could thus be:

> kommst du ´mit / ins The´ater?

This would have the effect of making the utterance appear to
contain two 'points' rather than one, where the second is added as
a kind of further remark, question, or elaboration. In the majority of
cases, however, we will find that the versions with a single intonation
group are the more normal.

This is not necessarily true for *all* utterances consisting of a single
clause, however. A number of special cases require mention where it
is more usual to divide the utterance into more than one intonation

group. The most important of these cases are those involving *apposition* and '*Ausrahmung*'.

Apposition

Appositional phrases are of several types. The distinction we are concerned with here is between 'defining' (or restrictive) and 'non-defining' (non-restrictive) apposition. For example, the utterance:

> Kennst du meinen Bruder, den Arzt?

has more than one interpretation according to whether the speaker has more than one brother or not. If the apposition is *defining*, the appositional phrase *den Arzt* serves to identify this one brother from among several (*meinen Bruder den Arzt, nicht meinen Bruder den Rechtsanwalt*), but if it is *non-defining* it simply adds further information about a brother whose identity is already established. (*Kennst du meinen Bruder? Er ist Arzt.*)

The significance of this particular distinction for intonation is that there is a regular difference in the number of intonation groups that are likely to be found in the utterance in these cases. Since with the defining type the appositional phrase belongs closely together with its antecedent (*Bruder*) as an integral part of the same phrase, it is not usual to divide such utterances up into more than one intonation group. With the non-defining type on the other hand, the appositional phrase is not so much an integral part of the same expression as an additional, and parallel phrase, and in this case it is usual to pronounce the utterance with a separate intonation group for the appositional phrase. Typical renderings of the two versions would thus be:

> (*defining*) kennst du meinen Bruder den ´Arzt?
> (*non-defining*) kennst du meinen ´Bruder / den ´Arzt?

The same principles apply to the following examples:

> frag mal `Heinrich / den Ex`perten!
> wie geht's deinem `Freund / `Dieter?
> er wohnt in `diesem Haus / dem `weißen.

Ausrahmung

Many German sentences are built on the so-called 'frame' pattern ('Rahmen'). Where there is more than one part to the verb (e.g. with auxiliary and participle, verb and separable prefix, and so on) the inflected part of the verb goes in its usual place near the beginning (in either first or second position according to the type of sentence) while the remainder goes to the end, thus enclosing most of the sentence in a kind of 'frame'. But it frequently happens that this principle is not rigidly observed, so that the final part of the verb is brought forward, with one or more parts of the sentence *after* it. This phenomenon is called *Ausrahmung* (the term *Ausklammerung* is also sometimes used). Examples are:

> ich habe mich beworben um diese Stelle
> er hat es gelesen in der Zeitung
> sie muß aufgeben wegen ihrer Krankheit

This kind of construction is important for intonation because in cases of *Ausrahmung* the utterance is regularly divided up into more than one intonation group, one for the main part of the sentence until the end of the 'frame', and one for the remaining items which are excluded from the 'frame'. Compare, for example, the following versions:

> er hat es in der `Zeitung gelesen
> er hat es ge`lesen / in der `Zeitung

This treatment of utterances with *Ausrahmung* is again explicable in terms of the division of utterances into 'information' units, and again we see how the grammatical structure of the utterance can collaborate, as it were, with intonation in order to produce a specific effect. *Ausrahmung* has the effect of breaking an utterance into two parts, with the matter excluded from the frame being treated as a kind of appendix to the main sentence, separate from it to some extent. This separate status is reflected in the division into intonation groups, which reinforces the syntactic division.

It must be stated once more that such divisions into intonation groups that we see in the case of apposition and *Ausrahmung* are not obligatory, but simply the most *likely* in view of the nature of the grammatical structure. The speaker may often override such considerations. A version such as:

> er hat es gelesen in der `Zeitung

though less expected than the version with two intonation groups, is in no way 'deviant' or 'wrong'. Intonation is rarely completely constrained by the grammatical structure of the utterance.

Appositional phrases are usually treated in exactly the same way in English and German, with the likelihood of a separate intonation group for the 'non-defining' type, e.g.

there's Mr `Smith / my next-door `neighbour

There is, of course, no direct equivalent of 'Ausrahmung' in English; many English-speakers who have learnt their German grammar 'properly' may not use 'Ausrahmung' much, if at all, in speaking German, but they should be aware that when it is used it sounds more natural with a separate intonation group for the excluded matter.

There are other cases where the number of intonation groups in utterances may be different in English and German. One of them is the treatment of the beginning of the sentence. As a general rule it may be said that both languages tend to put the subject of the sentence at the beginning. Indeed, in English, not to do so generally implies considerable contrast or emphasis. Thus, in the following cases:

(a) I read Buddenbrooks in April
(b) in April I read Buddenbrooks
(c) Buddenbrooks I read in April

(a) can be regarded as the normal version, while (b) and (c) are used for special effects. The type of structure represented by (b), in which an adverbial expression is put first, is quite common, but a version which puts the object first, as in (c), is unusual, and it might require some ingenuity to think of a suitable context in which such an utterance would sound natural.

In German, as is well known, the situation is somewhat different, since there is much greater flexibility with regard to what is put in the first position in the sentence, and, whatever the first item, the verb retains its second position (in English the subject–verb order is the same whatever goes first). Examples are:

(a) Ich habe Buddenbrooks im April gelesen
(b) im April habe ich Buddenbrooks gelesen
(c) Buddenbrooks habe ich im April gelesen

The first version (a) is the most straightforward, though (b) sounds almost as natural; (c) is not the most usual version but it is certainly in no way peculiar, and utterances with this structure are quite frequent.

In short, then, German is much more tolerant of various kinds of element in the first position of sentences, and replacement of the subject by some other part of the sentence is a much more regular, and less disruptive process than in English. Hence the effect of such a change in word order in English is often to separate off the element put at the beginning, to isolate it from the rest of the sentence to some extent, whereas in German this isolation is less marked, and indeed may not be evident at all.

Again this is reflected in the intonation. As we have seen in other cases, such as apposition and 'Ausrahmung', parts of the sentence which are separated off in some way tend to be pronounced with a separate intonation group, and the same applies here: in English in particular, items other than the subject at the beginning generally constitute a separate intonation group. In German, where items may appear more freely in first position in the sentence without being isolated from the rest, the tendency to give them a separate intonation group is less strong.

The expected versions of the above English examples would thus be as follows:

    (a) I read Buddenbrooks in `April
    (b) in ´April / I read `Buddenbrooks
    (c) ˜Buddenbrooks / I read in `April

while the German examples are likely to remain undivided:

    (a) ich habe Buddenbrooks im `April gelesen
    (b) im April habe ich `Buddenbrooks gelesen
    (c) Buddenbrooks habe ich im `April gelesen

In none of these cases, either in German or English, is this particular version obligatory. The first English example could easily be divided:

    I read ´Buddenbrooks / in `April

or the last example could be pronounced as a single intonation group:

    Buddenbrooks I read in `April

and similarly with the German examples. The differences between the two languages here are therefore to be found in the tendencies *in respect of these different types of word order.*

But it is also important to note that these differences arise from the different principles governing word order in English and German; they do not arise from any difference in the way intonation is used.

In both languages the principles governing the number of intonation groups in an utterance are the same: each intonation group constitutes a single unit of 'information', a communicative entity. Though we may in principle choose how many such units to use in either language, this choice may be influenced by the grammatical structure of the utterance. Certain types of structure, such as 'Ausrahmung' in German, initial elements which are not subjects in English, and non-defining appositional phrases in both languages, give to parts of the utterance a certain measure of communicative independence, and this is likely to be reinforced by their being treated as separate 'information' units and pronounced as separate intonation groups.

THE COMPLEX SENTENCE

While simple sentences are normally (except in the cases just mentioned) likely to constitute single intonation groups, complex sentences, with their greater grammatical complexity and greater length, are more likely to be divided into more than one intonation group. Different types of sentence differ in the extent to which they are likely to be construed as single or multiple units of 'information', however. The types which are of importance for intonation will be discussed in the remainder of this chapter.

Co-ordinate clauses

Co-ordinate clauses are normally given separate intonation groups:

> er hat ihr einen ⁻Brief geschrieben / aber sie hat ihn nicht geˋlesen
> ich habe schon ´dreimal bei ihr angerufen / und ich will es nicht
> ˋnoch einmal tun

This does not apply to sentences where only the verbs are co-ordinate, as in:

> er ißt und trinkt den ganzen ˋTag

Such sentences do not contain co-ordinate clauses, but a single clause with more than one verb. It would naturally be possible to divide up this sentence into two intonation groups, but the division would not normally separate the two verbs:

> er ißt und ´trinkt / den ganzen ˋTag

Some cases of this latter kind are, in fact, ambiguous, and intonation,

which may group parts of the utterance together as single communicative units, may serve to resolve the ambiguity. Consider, for example,
the following:

> er liest und schreibt Romane

This could mean that he reads other things besides novels, though
novels is all that he writes; or it could mean that both his reading and
writing are restricted to novels. That is, it could be a combination of
er liest (Bücher, Zeitungen, usw.) and *er schreibt Romane*, or of *er liest
Romane* and *er schreibt Romane*. The likely pronunciation in the
former case would be

> er ´liest / und schreibt Ro`mane

and in the latter

> er liest und schreibt Ro`mane

Relative clauses

Relative clauses are analogous to appositional phrases in a number of
respects. Like them, they are of two types, a 'defining' relative clause
which is a necessary part of the sentence, and a 'non-defining' relative
clause which is non-essential. Examples are:

> (*defining*) die Leute, die das glauben, sind verrückt
> (*non-defining*) Karl, der geschäftlich viel zu tun hat, ist verreist

Defining relative clauses, like defining appositional phrases, do not
normally form a separate intonation group, while non-defining ones
do. We would thus expect to find:

> die Leute, die das glauben, sind ver`rückt
> *or*
> die Leute, die das ´glauben / sind ver`rückt
> *but*
> ´Karl / der ge´schäftlich viel zu tun hat / ist ver`reist

As with appositional phrases, the explanation for this different
treatment evidently lies in the relative independence of the non-defining
type as a parallel expression to part of the main sentence.

Complement clauses

Complement clauses, such as those introduced by *daß* or *ob*, do not usually form a separate intonation group:

> ich weiß, daß er Sauerkraut nicht `leiden kann
> er hofft, daß es ihm diesmal ge`lingen wird
> weißt du, ob er noch ´da ist?

Substantival clauses

Substantival clauses (those which function like nouns) especially as the object of the sentence, do not usually form a separate intonation group:

> ich weiß nicht, was er `will
> sag mir, was ich zu `tun habe

But in many cases where English would have a substantival clause German prefers to use a (defining) relative clause:

> er interessiert sich nur für das, was seine `Freundin macht

> (*English*: he's only interested in what his girl-friend is doing)

In either case a single intonation group is likely.

Substantival clauses at the beginning of the sentence seem more susceptible to being given a separate intonation group:

> was er ´macht / macht er `falsch

(here *was* is equivalent to *was immer*). Another version of this utterance where the substantival clause is the *subject* seems most natural *without* a separate intonation group, however:

> was er macht ist `falsch

It will be evident from this that general rules for such cases are almost impossible to state, but since a parallel situation exists in English, the learner is unlikely to go seriously wrong.

Adverbial clauses

Whether adverbial clauses form a separate intonation group or not depends partly on where they occur. If they *follow* the main clause they are less likely to than if they *precede*:

ich fahre nie, wenn viel Ver`kehr ist
wenn viel Ver´kehr ist / fahre ich `nie

But again such tendencies are subject to considerable variation.

Tag questions

Although not, in German at least, strictly in the form of a clause, tag questions can be treated as such in view of their grammatical independence from the rest of the sentence. We have already noted in our discussion of types of intonation group sequences that tag questions regularly have a separate intonation group:

es ist `schön / ´nicht wahr?
Sie fahren `mit / ´oder?

The intonational independence of tag questions is no doubt a reflection of their separate communicative status: they do not form part of the rest of the sentence but are additional to it.

Despite an appearance of arbitrariness in the treatment of individual types of clause within complex sentences, the basic principles involved are clear enough, and are the same as those described in connection with simple sentences. Whether or not a part of a sentence is treated as a separate intonation group depends on its relative communicative independence within the sentence: the more independent it is, the more likely it is to be pronounced as a separate intonation group. Again, certain types of grammatical relationship within the sentence are conducive to the creation of such independence: co-ordinate clauses and tag questions are evidently of this type, as are non-defining relative clauses. On the other hand, the grammatical independence of a part of the sentence as a separate clause is no guarantee of its independence for the purposes of intonation, and certain types of clause – complement and defining relative clauses in particular – are evidently too much an integral part of the sentence and too closely linked to other parts to be treated as an independent communicative entity under normal circumstances, while other types of clauses, such as adverbial or substantival clauses, are of more variable status. And in all cases, of course, the speaker may easily override these principles and produce versions with a different number of intonation groups from the ones given here as 'normal'. These 'normal' correspondences thus constitute simply guide-lines rather than hard and fast rules.

13
The Meanings of Intonation
Group Sequences

In chapter 7 we considered commonly occurring sequences of intonation groups. The basic types discussed were the following:

1. High-ending + low-ending
   (level or rise + fall or rise–fall)
2. Low-ending + low-ending
   (fall or rise–fall + fall or rise–fall)
3. Low-ending + high-ending
   (fall or rise–fall + rise)
4. High-ending + high-ending
   (rise + rise)

These basic types can, as explained and exemplified in chapter 7, be
expanded into longer sequences with a similar structure by the addition
of further intonation groups.

LINKING

Sequences of the kinds listed here do not simply consist of an arbitrary
succession of intonation groups. The intonation groups in the sequence
are joined together, or linked to one another, so that the sequence
becomes a unified whole. In very many cases, the intonation groups
will also be linked together grammatically, because they form part
of the same sentence, but this is not always the case. The following
utterance, for example, consists of two separate sentences with no
grammatical connection between them, yet it forms a single entity
from the point of view of intonation:

er kommt ⁻morgen; er hat es mir ver`sprochen

In cases such as this, it is the intonation sequence itself which joins
together the parts of the utterance. The sequence has a *linking* function
which is independent of the grammatical connections between its parts.

TYPES OF LINKING

The links between the intonation groups in sequences can be of different kinds. In the above example we have two intonation groups, the first with a level pattern and the second with a fall. The level pattern in the first intonation group suggests to the listener that the utterance is not yet concluded: something more is to follow, and it is this that makes us feel that the two intonation groups belong together as a single entity, despite their grammatical independence. The first intonation group is incomplete in itself, and requires another intonation group to complete the intonational 'sense'. The second intonation group with the falling pattern does not create this impression of incompleteness, and does not require another intonation group to follow it.

The two intonation groups in this sequence are therefore of different kinds. One is 'incomplete', or *dependent*, and the other is 'complete', or *independent*. Independent intonation groups are self-sufficient and may stand alone, while dependent intonation groups need to be supplemented by another intonation group. This distinction is analogous to the grammatical distinction between 'main' and 'subordinate' clauses: the former are independent, the latter dependent. But again it is important to note that there is no necessary correspondence between the two. In the above example, *both* the clauses are main, yet from the point of view of intonation only the second intonation group is independent.

'Dependent' is also not to be equated with 'non-final'. Consider the following example:

> er kommt `morgen / weil er es mir ver`sprochen hat

In this sequence (here there is a low-ending pattern in both intonation groups) the first intonation group, though non-final, does not convey an impression of incompleteness at all, and must thus be regarded as independent. The second intonation group, though of course it is grammatically subordinate, is, from the point of view of intonation, likewise independent.

In these two examples, then, we find different kinds of relationship between the intonation groups in the sequence. In the first example we have a dependent intonation group followed by an independent one, and their relationship is one of *subordination*: the first intonation group is incomplete without, and therefore subordinated to, the second. But in the second example *both* intonation groups are independent, and their relationship is one of *co-ordination*.

Intonational subordination and co-ordination must be kept apart from grammatical subordination and co-ordination. The two are completely independent. Consider the following examples:

> wenn das ⁻Wetter schlecht ist / können wir nicht ˋausgehen
> wie ich die ⁻Tür aufmachte / war niemand mehr zu ˋsehen

Both of these utterances consist of a dependent intonation group followed by an independent one, and here this is completely parallel to the grammatical structure, since the first clause is subordinate in each case, and the second clause is main. But this correspondence is not at all necessary. To demonstrate this we need only reverse the order of the clauses while keeping the intonation structure intact:

> wir können nicht ⁻ausgehen / wenn das ˋWetter schlecht ist
> es war niemand mehr zu ⁻sehen / wie ich die ˋTür aufmachte

Here the first clause is grammatically main, but the first intonation group is subordinated to the second.

THE MEANING OF SUBORDINATION AND CO-ORDINATION

In the last chapter we saw that the intonation group can be regarded as a communicative unit, a single piece of 'information', and that utterances containing more than one intonation group will consist of more than one such unit. The examples given so far in this chapter show that the intonation groups in sequences may be either dependent or independent. What is the significance of this for their status as units of 'information'?

Dependence and independence of intonation groups is not just a matter of 'incompleteness' and 'completeness', but has wider implications for communication. In sequences containing both types of intonation group the independent intonation group is communicatively more significant; it constitutes the main 'point' of the utterance, while the dependent intonation group gives subordinate information, information which may have been mentioned before, is already known, is assumed or taken for granted, or is otherwise less important than that found in the independent intonation group. Let us consider once again some of the examples given previously:

> wenn das ⁻Wetter schlecht ist / können wir nicht ˋausgehen
> wir können nicht ⁻ausgehen / wenn das ˋWetter schlecht ist

The assumptions implicit in each of these utterances are different. The first example takes the condition for granted and makes a point about the consequences; the second assumes the consequences and makes a point about the conditions under which they would be true. In one sense, of course, the 'content' of the two sentences is the same, and the grammatical relationships are also identical in the two cases, but the different order of the clauses, coupled with the subordinating intonation structure, gives a different communicative effect: in each case the main point is contained in the independent intonation group.

This difference in meaning is also evident from the kinds of questions to which these two utterances could constitute answers. The question *Was geschieht, wenn das Wetter schlecht ist?* could only be answered in a natural way with the first example, whereas only the second example would do as an answer to the question *Wann können wir nicht ausgehen?* To use the second example as an answer to the first question, or the first example as an answer to the second question would make nonsense of the whole conversation, and we would feel that communication between the speakers had broken down.

Another way of showing that the main communicative weight in these examples is in the second intonation group is to reduce the whole utterance to a single intonation group and see where the nucleus occurs in a communicatively equivalent version. If these examples are to retain their communicative value, the nucleus in the single intonation group would have to occur in the *second* part, e.g.:

> wenn das Wetter schlecht ist, können wir nicht ˋausgehen
> wir können nicht ausgehen, wenn das ˋWetter schlecht ist

Though less natural than the versions with two intonation groups, these could be used to answer the same questions without implying a breakdown in communication. Putting the nucleus in the *first* part, on the other hand, would again make nonsense of the conversation:

> wenn das ˋWetter schlecht ist, können wir nicht ausgehen
> wir können nicht ˋausgehen, wenn das Wetter schlecht ist

Though perfectly natural utterances, these can no longer be used to answer the same questions. The first could now be an answer to the second question, *Wann können wir nicht ausgehen?* and the second an answer to the first question, *Was geschieht, wenn das Wetter schlecht ist?*

Yet another way of making the same point about the greater communicative importance of the second intonation group in such sequences is to omit the dependent intonation group entirely. Again the communicative value of the full version is preserved, since these abbreviated versions could be used as answers to the same questions:

> wir können nicht `ausgehen
> wenn das `Wetter schlecht ist

The first example is again appropriate as an answer to the question *Was geschieht, wenn das Wetter schlecht ist*? and the second is appropriate for the question *Wann können wir nicht ausgehen*?

In these examples the relationship between the intonation groups is that of subordination, with one intonation group dependent on the other. In sequences where the intonation groups are in a co-ordinating relationship the communicative values are also different. Consider the following examples:

> er kommt `morgen / weil er es mir ver`sprochen hat
> es war niemand mehr zu `sehen / wie ich die `Tür aufmachte
> wir können nicht `ausgehen / wenn das `Wetter schlecht ist

Although utterances such as these may appear to be less natural than those discussed so far, they are in fact extremely common in normal conversation. Here, the first intonation group, as noted above, does not give the impression of incompleteness that the initial intonation groups of the subordinating sequences do, and *both* intonation groups can be regarded as independent. From the communicative point of view, we find that neither can be treated as conveying the main point of the utterance; instead, the impression is of *two* such points, the second being additional to, rather than subordinated to, the first. (Again we must not be misled by the *grammatically* subordinate status of the second part.)

This is also reflected in the possibility of using these utterances as answers to questions. Since two points are being made, these utterances do not sound natural when the preceding question already contains one of the points. Thus, the last of the above examples is inappropriate as an answer to *both* the question *Was geschieht, wenn das Wetter schlecht ist*? *and* the question *Wann können wir nicht ausgehen*? The unnaturalness lies in the fact that one of the intonation groups (the second in the case of the first question, and the first in the case of the second question) is making a point that is already made by the question itself.

Similarly, it is not possible to reduce co-ordinate sequences to a single intonation group, wherever we put the nucleus, nor to omit one of the intonation groups, while retaining the communicative value of the utterance. This would change the status of the information contained in the intonation group whose nucleus is lost or which is omitted; it becomes subordinate.

In short, then, we can see that the distinction between dependent and independent intonation groups is an important one. It reflects the communicative value of the various parts of the utterance. Those parts of an utterance which are contained in an independent intonation group constitute a main point, a significant contribution to the conversation, while those parts that are contained in a dependent intonation group are communicatively subordinate.

COMMUNICATIVE TYPE AND SEQUENCE TYPE

It is possible to relate co-ordinating and subordinating types of intonation structures to the types of sequences summarized at the beginning of this chapter in a fairly consistent way. Certain types of sequence, in other words, are regularly co-ordinating and others regularly subordinating.

High-ending + low ending

This is the characteristic *subordinating* sequence, and all the examples of subordination given above are of this type. The first, high-ending, intonation group is dependent on the second. Here are some more examples:

> er hat mir er ´zählt / daß er sein `Haus verkauft hat
> meine ¯Mutter ist krank / und ich muß nach `München fahren
> warum er nicht er¯schienen ist / `weiß ich nicht

Low-ending + low ending

This is the characteristic *co-ordinating* sequence, and all the cases of co-ordinate intonation groups given above have had a low-ending pattern in both intonation groups. Further examples are:

> ich habe meinen `Hut verloren / den `grauen
> ich muß nach `Hause gehen / bevor es `dunkel wird
> ich fahre nächste `Woche / nach Ber`lin

Here, the two intonation groups constitute communicative units of equal value, each making a separate point. In some cases this gives the impression of an afterthought; the second point is an elaboration or further clarification of the first.

Low-ending + high ending

In this type of sequence, which occurs characteristically in sentences containing tag questions, the final high-ending pattern does not convey the same impression of dependence as the high-ending pattern in the first intonation group of the high + low sequence. The low-ending pattern of the first intonation group indicates, as before, that this part of the utterance constitutes a main point, but the second intonation group is equally significant, though in a different way. We can therefore treat this type of sequence as parallel in its communicative value to the low + low sequence, i.e. as co-ordinate, though the implication of the rising pattern in the second intonation group is naturally rather different from that of the fall in the low + low sequence, since it gives the end of the utterance a note of 'appeal' (see chapter 9, above). Utterances which contain this type of sequence thus contain two points, one of which is an 'assertion' and the other an 'appeal'. This parallels the syntactic structure of sentences of this kind, in which a declarative clause is followed by an interrogative element (in German usually without a verb and therefore not a full clause). Here are some further examples:

> er heißt `Müller / ´nicht?
> sie arbeitet in der Bäcker`ei / ´oder?

High-ending + high-ending

This type of sequence is not only relatively uncommon, it is also not quite as straightforward as the others. In the majority of cases the communicative values of the intonation groups are the same as those of the low + low sequence, i.e. co-ordinating. Repetition of intonation patterns in successive intonation groups is, in fact, a regular way of indicating communicative equivalence. The overall implication of such sentences is naturally different from that of the low + low sequence because of the rising pattern, but the relationship between the intonation groups is the same. Further examples are:

> kommen Sie ´mit / in die `Stadt?
> darf ich eine ´Frage stellen / eine ´kurze?

The parallel between the low + low and the high + high sequences can be demonstrated by converting one to the other. Thus, if we take an instance of the former, and change the 'assertion' into an 'appeal', we must change the pattern in *both* intonation groups:

> das ist Herr `Müller / der Di`rektor

becomes:

> das ist Herr ´Müller / der Di´rektor?

This co-ordinate status of the intonation groups when pronounced with a high + high sequence does not always hold true, however. It is possible to have an initial intonation group subordinated not only to a following intonation group with a low-ending pattern (as in the high + low sequence) but also to a following intonation group with a high-ending pattern, and in this case the first intonation group will have a rising pattern, but it will be dependent on the second. Examples are:

> wenn es ´schön ist / wollen Sie ´mitkommen?
> gestern ´Abend / hat es viel ge´regnet?

Similarly, converting the assertion of an utterance with an initial subordinate intonation group (i.e. with a high + low sequence) into an appeal, will result in a high + high sequence:

> der Mann mit der roten Kra´watte / das ist Herr `Müller

becomes:

> der Mann mit der roten Kra´watte / das ist Herr ´Müller?

The high + high sequence thus has two interpretations. It may be a co-ordinating structure, parallel to the low + low sequence, or it may be a subordinating structure, parallel to the high + low sequence. Only the context will determine which interpretation is appropriate.

As a general conclusion from this discussion of the types of sequences, we may note that the choice of sequence has considerable communicative significance. By choosing a *subordinating* sequence we make one part of the utterance of lesser communicative status than the other; there is a main point and a secondary one. With a *co-ordinating* sequence, on the other hand, we create *two* main points, of equal communicative value. This choice of different communicative structures is independent of the *grammatical* status of the parts of the utterance.

English intonation group sequences can be treated in an analogous fashion, with high-ending and low-ending patterns having a similar function. The range of high-ending patterns is wider, as we have seen, but the basic function of these pattern types is the same. Thus, in addition to the rise + fall and the level + fall of German we also find a rise–fall–rise + fall and a low rise + fall sequence. In all these cases the first high-ending pattern is subordinate and the second low-ending pattern is main.

There is one type of English sequence which requires more specific mention, however: where a low-ending pattern is followed by a high-ending pattern, and where the latter is either a rise–fall–rise or a low rise. These do not occur in German, as was noted in chapter 7, but this absence is particularly important because it constitutes a significant structural *difference between the two languages, which has implications for the meaning of intonation in the two languages.*

Consider first the following examples:

1. I've got to go to ˋBirmingham / on ͵Wednesday
2. she can be quite ˋnice to me / when it ͵suits her
3. you can take it ˆwith you / if you ˜like

(͵ represents the low rise and ˜ the rise–fall–rise).
In these examples it seems clear that the main communicative weight lies in the first *intonation group rather than in the second, the latter constituting a secondary addition of subordinate status. To provide evidence of this we may reverse the word order and attempt to obtain a similar communicative content; this will result in our using a high-ending pattern in the first intonation group and a low-ending pattern in the second:*

1(a)   on ˜Wednesday / I've got to go to ˋBirmingham
2(a)   when it ˜suits her / she can be quite ˋnice to me
3(a)   if you ˜like / you can take it ˆwith you

In other words, there is near equivalence, from the communicative point of view, of (1) and (1a), (2) and (2a), and (3) and (3a). Compare this, however, with versions in which the status of the intonation groups is reversed, without changing the order:

1(b)   I've got to go to ˜Birmingham / on ˋWednesday
2(b)   she can be quite ˜nice to me / when it ˋsuits her
3(b)   you can take it ˜with you / if you ˆlike

The meaning of (1b) is now quite different from that of (1) or (1a), even though the word order is the same as that of (1).

We may say, therefore, that in a sequence of intonation groups in English with a fall or rise-fall in the first intonation group and a low rise or a rise–fall–rise in the second the first intonation group will be main and the second subordinate. This kind of structure is one which is not found in German. The difference between the two languages at this point is not simply that English has a few extra patterns in certain types of intonation groups, but that English has a wider range of intonation structures than German. In English, it is possible for a subordinate intonation group to follow *a main one, but in German a subordinate intonation group must* precede *a main one.*

This difference is particularly important because the structure in question is a very frequent one in English. English is able to present subordinate pieces of information of this sort after the main piece of information. Subordinate expressions such as adverbs, qualifications, conditions, afterthoughts, etc., are regularly treated in this way, as in the above examples.

Now the communicative needs of German-speakers are in principle not likely to differ much from those of English-speakers, and we may well ask how Germans are able to convey the same kind of communicative 'weighting' as in this type of English structure. In fact, of course, we would not expect to find any direct equivalence between the various devices available in different languages for this kind of purpose, but it is possible to make a few observations about the way in which German might be said to make good this 'deficiency' in its intonation structures.

We have already observed (in chapter 12) that English and German differ to some extent in the freedom with which they are able to place different parts of the sentence at the beginning. German is more tolerant of such items as direct objects in initial position, since they are more easily accommodated here and integrated into the sentence by inverting the subject and the verb. In English, placing such items at the beginning is a much more disruptive process, and, as we have seen, this is reflected in the greater tendency to isolate them intonationally, by pronouncing them with a separate intonation group. This is less frequent in German.

These differences between the two languages may be seen as to a certain extent complementary. English is able to obtain greater flexibility and variety by its intonational treatment of final *expressions;*

German, on the other hand, exploits initial *position more fully, but without using intonation. It would be unjustifiable and misleading to relate these two characteristics in any detailed and consistent fashion. Nevertheless an English utterance such as:*

I'm buying a new `car / to ˌmorrow

might be aptly compared with the German:

morgen kaufe ich mir ein neues `Auto

with the subordinate prominence of 'tomorrow / morgen' effected in different ways in the two languages.

This parallel between the two languages, where similar communicative needs are met in rather different ways, will be found to hold for many cases, but there are inevitably instances where the equivalence cannot be achieved without seriously distorting the utterance in other respects. One such case is the so-called 'comment clause', i.e. expressions such as 'I think', 'I believe', etc. In both languages these are most naturally tagged on to the end of an utterance as a kind of reservation or qualification. In English, the most natural way of treating these expressions is to make them into a separate intonation group of subordinate status and hence with a low rising or rising-falling-rising pattern.*

he'll be coming to `morrow / I supˌpose
she must be over `forty / I should ˜think

In German no such possibility exists, but such expressions cannot be readily transported to the beginning of the sentence without destroying their character as an afterthought. In these cases, then, we find the equivalent German utterance without *a separate intonation group.*

er kommt `morgen, nehm'ich an
sie muß über `vierzig sein, glaub'ich

A similar problem arises with 'postponed' items, especially subjects or objects, as in:

they're always com`plaining / these ˌstudents
I've already `met him / the new ˌteacher

Again German cannot separate these off as a separate intonation group.

sie be`klagen sich immer, diese Studenten
ich `kenne ihn schon, den neuen Lehrer

The implications of these differences are far-reaching, since here it is not simply a matter of avoiding a particular pattern or modifying one's general pitch behaviour. In this case it is a whole type of structure *that must be avoided by the English learner of German. The English-speaker has a natural tendency to use a low-rising (or, less often, a rising–falling–rising) pattern for final subordinate items such as those discussed here. In order to obtain something approaching an equivalent utterance in German he must acquire the habit of organizing his sentences differently, so that no subordinate elements to which it is desirable to give some sort of prominence are left in final position; the prominence must be achieved by other means, notably by placing the items in question at the beginning.*

LONGER SEQUENCES

As we saw in chapter 7, these basic types of intonation group sequences containing only two intonation groups can be extended by the addition of an indefinite number of further intonation groups. The different types of sequence may be extended in different ways: the high-ending + low-ending sequence may be lengthened by the addition of further high-ending patterns before the final fall or rise–fall; the low-ending + low-ending and the high-ending + high-ending patterns may be extended by repetition of the low or high-ending pattern respectively, while the low-ending + high-ending sequence (with a final high rise) may have more than one low-ending pattern before the rise.

In all these cases exactly the same principles are seen to be at work as in the case of simpler sequences. Again we may recognize subordinate and main intonation groups and extensions may involve having more than one of these types within the same sequence. Consider the following examples:

1. wenn der ⁻Klaus kommt / können wir ihn ´fragen /ob er `mitkommen will
2. ich kann ja leider nicht `bleiben / weil ich meinen `Freund / noch `abholen muß
3. er kann sowohl Chi´nesisch / als auch Ja`panisch / was mir ungeheuer impo`niert
4. Sie haben doch in ´München / ziemlich `lange gelebt / ´nicht?

In example (1) we have the sequence high + high + low, where the high-ending patterns are subordinate and the final low-ending pattern is main. This sort of sequence can be extended almost indefinitely by the addition of still further high-ending patterns. This is characteristic of rather formal reading aloud of prepared speeches, where there are fairly long sentences, and the speaker continues with high-ending patterns until the end of the sentence allows him to conclude with a main intonation group. Example (2), on the other hand, is more characteristic of informal speech. This consists of a sequence of low-ending patterns, which again may be extended as long as necessary. The fact that every intonation group is treated as main makes this kind of sequence frequent in unprepared speaking, where the speaker is continually adding further 'main points' to his utterances, without necessarily being clear as to where his utterance is going or when it will stop.

Examples (3) and (4) illustrate combinations of subordinate and main intonation groups. (3) begins with high-ending and a low-ending pattern and adds an additional low pattern, making two main points and one subordinate one, while (4) has a similar structure but with a final tag question. Many more different combinations on similar lines could easily be given. They all follow the same basic principles.

SEQUENCES AND GRAMMATICAL STRUCTURE

It is difficult to give any precise rules for determining the kind of sequence that a speaker will use in any particular case since, as we have seen, the choice depends on the relative communicative weight that the speaker wishes to give to the various parts of his utterance, and what is, in the context in question, the chief communicative point. There clearly can be no mechanical procedure for determining this from the grammatical structure of the sentence. Nevertheless, as with other features of intonation which are similarly independent of grammar, it is possible to identify certain types of grammatical element which may be *likely* to be treated in a certain way unless there is good reason not to. Any statements to this effect must, of course, be treated with caution, and not adhered to slavishly; here is a case where the speaker's intuitive judgements are likely to be of more service to him than any rules.

Given a series of intonation groups forming a sequence, we might surmise that what determines whether this sequence will consist of main or subordinate intonation groups (there must always be at least *one* main intonation group, of course) will be the extent to which the grammatical construction concerned provides equivalent or parallel pieces of information, which the speaker is thus likely to treat as conveying points of equivalent importance. This is, broadly speaking, the case; it is possible to identify a number of constructions, or parts of sentences of certain types, which do seem regularly to be treated as either main or subordinate. As a general rule it is probably true to say that sequences will contain only one main intonation group (the last) *unless there is some specific reason for the contrary*. Among the cases where there *is* such a reason are the following: apposition, non-defining relative clauses, sentential relative clauses, and tag questions.

Apposition

Cases of non-defining apposition are, as we saw in the previous chapter, regularly given a separate intonation group. Where the antecedent is part of a main intonation group, the appositional phrase is also likely to be main:

> bringen Sie bitte den `Stuhl herein / den `großen
> kennen Sie Herrn ´Scholz / den ´Rechtsanwalt?
> wo ist der `andere / der mit der `Brille?

But where the antecedent is in a subordinate intonation group, the appositional phrase is likely to follow suit:

> der ´andere / der mit der ´Brille / ist nicht ge`kommen

Relative clauses

Relative clauses are entirely parallel to appositional phrases in their intonation. We have seen that they will take a separate intonation group if non-defining, and whether this intonation group is main or subordinate will depend on the antecedent:

> ich habe Fraülein `Bäcker eingeladen / die mit mir in Ber`lin war
> hast du seinen letzten Ro´man gelesen / den er in A´merika schrieb?
> Fräulein ´Bäcker / die mit mir in Ber´lin war / habe ich `auch
>   eingeladen
> seinen letzten Ro´man / den er in A´merika schreib / ist sehr
>   `lohnend

Sentential relative clauses

Sentential relative clauses resemble ordinary relative clauses in some respects, but differ in that their antecedent is a whole clause. They regularly have a parallel intonation to their antecedent clause:

er `trinkt zu viel / was mich sehr be`ängstigt
der neue Chef hat viel Er´fahrung / was ungeheuer `wichtig ist

Tag questions

The typical intonation pattern of tag questions has already been discussed several times. Both the main sentence and the tag question will regularly constitute main intonation groups, i.e. there will be a co-ordinate structure. A peculiarity of this construction is, however, that the patterns in the two intonation groups are generally different, with a low-ending pattern in the first intonation group and a high-ending pattern (a rise) in the second. Another possibility is to have a low-ending pattern in *both* intonation groups, but this is very restricted (see chapter 14, where this is explored more fully).

The various types of grammatical element which are likely to be treated as main rather than subordinate have one characteristic in common: they form parts of utterances which are in some way *parallel* to other parts, rather than being subordinate to them. Parallelism of grammatical structure results in parallelism of intonational structure.

These examples are, of course, only characteristic cases where the grammatical structure has an influence on the communicative structure of the utterance. But it must be emphasized that such correspondences between intonation and grammatical structure are not obligatory; the speaker may frequently deviate from them according to the communicative demands of a specific context. Cases such as the above are not always treated as co-ordinate, and other types of construction which might be expected to have a subordinating intonation structure are not infrequently found with co-ordinate intonation groups.

The basic principles at work here are by no means peculiar to German; they determine to an equal extent the structure of intonation sequences in English, though the range of intonation structures in English is slightly larger. Similar kinds of grammatical element are likely to be treated in a similar way, though with the same reservation that the speaker may choose to deviate from the general principles. Thus we find that appositional phrases and relative clauses will be main or subordinate under exactly the same conditions in both languages, and both sentential relative clauses and tag questions will be regularly main.

14
The Meanings of Patterns
in Sequences

We have so far considered sequences of intonation groups in terms of two types of pattern, high-ending and low-ending, and in terms of the status of the intonation groups as either independent or dependent. We may now proceed to a consideration of the significance of the individual patterns for the meaning of the sequence.

THE ROLE OF INDEPENDENT INTONATION GROUPS

Sequences of the sort that we have been discussing form a meaningful whole; the intonation groups belong together as part of the same piece of communication. The basic character of the meaning of the sequence as a whole is determined by the independent intonation group or groups that it contains. Thus, if we take a single independent intonation group such as the following:

> wir können ihn be˙suchen

we can expand it by the addition of dependent intonation groups:

> wenn wir ´wollen / können wir ihn be˙suchen
> ‾morgen / wenn wir ‾wollen / können wir ihn be˙suchen

but these dependent intonation groups do not affect the basic meaning of the sequence as a whole, which, in this case, remains that of an *assertion*. Similarly, if the independent intonation group has a rising pattern, the element of *appeal* is likewise the basic meaning of the sequence as a whole:

> wenn wir ´wollen / können wir ihn be´suchen?

Thus the independent intonation group dominates the sequence; it gives its meaning to the whole sequence. (Attention is drawn to the discussion of the significance of the terms 'assertion' and 'appeal' in chapter 9, above.)

CO-ORDINATING SEQUENCES

Apart from the case of tag questions, where a low-ending pattern is regularly followed by a high-ending one, an important characteristic of co-ordinating sequences is that they have the same type of pattern — high-ending or low-ending — in all their independent intonation groups. This parallelism of pattern type reflects their equivalent status as the main communicative 'points' in the utterance. This parallelism frequently goes even further, so that it is usual to have not just the same *type* of pattern (high-ending or low-ending) but also the same specific nuclear pattern (fall, rise-fall) and not infrequently even the same variant of a specific pattern. The following are thus typical co-ordinate sequences:

er ist `krank / und seine Mutter `auch
das ˆglaub ich dir nicht / weil er die ganze Zeit ˆhier war
trinkst du gern Kaf´fee / oder ´Tee?

The parallelism of specific patterns is not obligatory, however, and it is perfectly natural to say:

er ist `krank / und seine Mutter ˆauch

or:

er ist ˆkrank / und seine Mutter `auch

The possibility of mixing different patterns in this way is in no way an exception to the principle that a sequence is a meaningful whole, or that the meaning of the independent intonation groups determines the character of the whole sequence, since the patterns remain within the same type. Both the fall and the rise-fall, as low-ending patterns, have the same basic implication of an assertion, and there is thus no conflict between them. The rise-fall adds an element of involvement or commitment to the intonation group in which it occurs.

TAG QUESTIONS

We have noted that tag questions regularly differ from other co-ordinating sequences in having two different types of pattern in their independent intonation groups (just as they differ grammatically from other types of co-ordinate sentence in having two different kinds of sentence in their main clauses). In this case, of course, there can be no constant meaning throughout; the first intonation group contains an assertive element, and the final tag an element of appeal:

> der Hund heißt `Bella / ´nicht?
> das Konzert war ˆhimmlisch / ´nicht wahr?

This is the typical form of a tag question in German, but it is not the only possibility. Though much rarer, a sequence of two rising patterns is also possible.

> Sie kommen ´mit / ´oder?

and, still more rarely, a sequence of two falls:

> Sie kommen nicht `mit / oder `doch?

English and German differ to some extent in the co-ordinating inton-ation sequences that they tend to give to tag questions. In English, tag questions usually contain a verb, and may be positive or negative, and there is a complex relationship between the positive or negative main sentence, a positive or negative tag, and the intonation pattern. Consider the following:

> 1(a) he's `done it / ´hasn't he?
> (b) he's `done it / `hasn't he?
> 2(a) he hasn't `done it / ´has he?
> (b) he hasn't `done it / `has he?
> 3(a) he's `done it / ´has he?

but not:

> (b) he's `done it / `has he?

Similarly, a fourth possibility, 'he hasn't done it, hasn't he?' though not impossible, seems to be rare with any intonation. A further possible rendering, as a single intonation group with a rising–falling–rising pattern, falls outside the present discussion of co-ordinate sequences:

> he hasn't ˜done it has he?

A detailed characterization of the differences between these various versions is left to the reader's ingenuity, but a few notes are appropri-ate. The basic type of tag question has a tag with the positive or nega-tive polarity of the main sentence reversed, and a rising pattern on the tag, as in (1a) and (2a). Here the main sentence presents an assumption, and the tag seeks to confirm it by asking if the reverse is, or is not, true. With a fall on the tag, as in (1b) and (2b) the tag itself takes on the character of an assertion, and thus reinforces rather than questions the original assumption. The truth of the assumption is thus taken more for granted in these versions.

A tag question in which the tag has the same polarity as the main sentence is only possible if both are positive, as in (3a). Here, the more assertive falling tag (3b) is also excluded.

In German the range of possibilities is more restricted, largely because the tag is grammatically quite different. The relationship between positive and negative polarity and the intonation pattern is less easy to establish. The main tags are 'nicht', 'nicht wahr', 'oder', 'oder nicht', 'oder doch', *though other forms, such as* 'gell', *are found regionally. The following are the chief possibilities:*

1. er hat es ge`macht / ´nicht (nicht wahr, oder nicht)?
2. er hat es nicht ge`macht / ´oder (oder doch)?
3. er hat es nicht ge`macht / oder `doch?

Though (1) and (2) may be equated with (1a) and (2a) of the English examples, there is no straightforward German equivalent of (1b) and (2b). The stronger assertion of these forms might be obtained by the insertion of 'doch' *into the main sentence (on the use of German particles and their relationship to English intonation patterns see the next chapter):*

er hat es doch ge`macht / ´nicht wahr?

Or the whole utterance may be reduced to a single intonation group, in which case the appeal element of the tag is virtually eliminated:

er hat es doch ge`macht nicht wahr?

Example (3) is perhaps not properly a tag question. It corresponds to an English version such as:

he hasn't `done it / or `has he?

SUBORDINATING SEQUENCES

The principal subordinating sequences given in chapter 13 were the following:

level + fall
rise + fall

    level + rise–fall
    rise + rise–fall
    rise + rise

(The rising pattern may also be of the fall–rise variety.)

We have already noted that the pattern of the independent intonation group (the second one) gives to the sequence as a whole its basic meaning. Hence the pattern or patterns of any dependent intonation groups do not affect this basic meaning, and sequences with the same pattern in the independent intonation group will have the same basic meaning whatever the pattern of the dependent intonation group. Nevertheless, the pattern of the dependent intonation group is not without significance. Consider the following examples:

    wenn es ⁻regnet / müssen wir mit dem `Bus fahren
    wenn es ´regnet / müssen wir mit dem `Bus fahren

These utterances differ only in the pattern of the first intonation group; their basic meaning is the same: both are assertions because of the falling pattern in the second intonation group. Nevertheless, they are not identical in meaning. In what way does their meaning differ?

The difference appears to lie in the nature of the connection between the two parts of the utterance. In both cases the high-ending pattern indicates the subordinate status of the first intonation group, but there are apparently different kinds of subordination. We could see the level + fall type as the basic form, conveying only the subordination of the first intonation group, while the rising pattern adds an extra element of meaning: it suggests that the connection between the parts is somewhat closer; the two parts are *complementary* to each other. It is no doubt for this reason that the sentences involving alternatives or contrasts tend to have a rise in the first intonation group:

    kommen Sie ´mit / oder bleiben Sie zu `Hause?
    ich war schon ´zweimal in Amerika / aber meine Frau nur `einmal
    er ist nicht er´schienen / aber die Sitzung hat `trotzdem stattge-
        funden

But these sentences are not restricted to this type of sequence, and a rise may occur in dependent intonation groups without such overt alternatives or contrast. The rise is used wherever it is desired to indicate the close or complementary connection between the parts.

The difference between the simple rise and the fall–rise was discussed in chapter 10. It was noted there that the fall–rise is a 'stronger' version of the rise which serves to give more prominence to the nucleus of the intonation group. This applies, too, when these forms are used in dependent intonation groups. Thus we may say:

im vorigen ˊWinter / waren wir in der ˋSchweiz

or

im vorigen ˇWinter / waren wir in der ˋSchweiz

and in the second version *Winter* is given more significance, perhaps as a contrast to *Sommer*.

Some German speakers appear to use the fall-rise form more widely in dependent intonation groups, however, especially in slower, more formal speech, such as reading aloud or lecturing. For them, the fall-rise may even be preferred to the simple rise or the level pattern in this style of speaking.

With a rising pattern in the independent intonation group, a preceding subordinate intonation group is relatively infrequent. The level pattern seems to be excluded here, so that we find only a rise (or a fall-rise):

wenn du ˇZeit hast / kommst du ˊmit?

Similar principles apply in English, but here the range of possibilities in dependent intonation groups is somewhat larger, because of the existence of the rising-falling-rising and low-rising patterns which do not exist in German. The level pattern is rather infrequent, but the rise-fall--rise and the low rise are extremely common. The major possibilities may be illustrated as follows:

if it ˌrains / we'll have to go by ˋbus
if it ˊrains / we'll have to go by ˋbus
if it ˇrains / we'll have to go by ˋbus
if it ˉrains / we'll have to go by ˋbus

Again the reader may attempt to characterize the differences in meaning for himself, and in doing so may come to realize how subtle the differences conveyed by intonation are, and how difficult it is to describe them. It might be possible to regard the low rise as the basic pattern here, while the rise-fall-rise has an additional implication, suggesting that the first part is a condition, reservation or prerequisite for the second rather than merely linked and subordinated to it. The high rise conveys a similar note of complementarity to its German counterpart.

Whatever interpretation we choose to give to these differences, however, the most important thing for the English learner to note is that he must suppress two of the patterns he commonly uses in dependent intonation groups: the low rise and the rise–fall–rise. Instead he must acquire the habit of using only the level or high-rising patterns of German. This will involve greater use of the level pattern than he is used to in English. Many cases where English-speakers would habitually use a rise–fall–rise will sound most natural in German with the high-rise rather than the level pattern.

15
Intonation and Modal Particles

In the preceding chapters we have examined in some detail the forms and functions of German intonation. In doing so we have considered intonation as a system of pitch features which are largely independent of other characteristics of utterances. Although it has often been found useful to relate intonation, however loosely, to such features as grammatical structure or word order, it will nevertheless be clear that there is no direct dependence of intonation on these features, and that the meaning of intonation is rather different from that of other parts of language.

There is one further characteristic of German sentences that calls for some discussion in this context: the so-called *modal particles*. These are the short 'filler' words like *doch*, *ja* and *denn*, which are frequently used in colloquial German to add particular shades of meaning to utterances. Since these shades of meaning seem, like those of intonation patterns, to reflect the speaker's attitude to what he is saying rather than constituting part of the content of the utterance as such, it is necessary for us to examine a little more closely the relationship between these particles and intonation.

Consideration of the relationship between these particles and intonation is also relevant for the English-speaking learner. We have noted on several occasions that, despite a fundamental and important parallel between the structure, patterns, and functions of intonation in the two languages, there are some differences, not only in the fine detail of the patterns but also in the set of patterns themselves and in the structures that they create. In particular there is no equivalent in German to two of the English patterns – the low rise and the rise-fall–rise – and one type of structure in which these patterns occur – an independent intonation group followed by a dependent one – is also lacking in German.

All this suggests that the German intonation system is less complex, less rich, than the English, and that consequently English relies more

heavily than German on intonation in conveying the meaning of utter-
ances. If this is so, then we may ask whether German has any other
features which might have a similar kind of role to that played by
intonation in English and which might therefore compensate for the
less rich intonation system.

We have, in fact, already noted the greater use made by German
of word order, particularly at the beginning of sentences, which can,
like intonation, indicate different degrees of prominence to be attached
to individual words or phrases (see p. 81, above). But another character-
istic of German sentences which might be considered relevant here is
the use of the modal particles. The temptation to see the German
particles as the equivalent of certain English intonation patterns is very
strong, particularly as English almost completely lacks particles of
this kind.

The relationship between intonation and modal particles is not
easy to establish, because the meaning of the particles, like the meaning
of intonation, is rather difficult to pin down. The shades of meaning
contributed by the particles are often difficult to express in any other
form. Furthermore, it is not always possible to say exactly which
words should be treated as modal particles, and whether or not a particular use of such a word is 'modal', as several of these words have
other, non-modal, uses, too. For example, the word *schon* is a straightforward temporal adverb in an utterance such as *ist er schon da?*, but
has no temporal connotations in *das ist schon wahr*, and its use here
may be considered modal.

In order to clarify the relationship between the modal particles
and intonation we must first attempt to characterize briefly the meanings or functions of the particles. The list of potential particles is quite
long, but here we shall restrict ourselves to the most important. Those
that we shall consider are *doch*, *ja*, *mal*, *denn*, *schon*, *eben*, *wohl*,
etwa and *auch*. Others that could be added are *nur* and *aber*, as well
as more independent words such as *eigentlich*, *allerdings*, *freilich*, and
nämlich, but the case for regarding these as modal particles is a little
less strong.

Doch

This particle is widely used when the speaker is contradicting a previous
utterance, usually a negative one, or when he is implying that the
previous utterance contains a false assumption. Examples are:

    das macht doch nichts
    das ist doch ganz natürlich

The implication here is that the previous speaker has assumed the contrary.

Ja

While *doch* draws attention to something which contradicts a previous assumption, *ja* points out something the listener can be expected to know or agree with, as in the following examples:

    er ist ja schon dreißig Jahre alt
    ich war ja auch in Frankreich

The implication here is that the information provided confirms or supports the listener's assumptions.

Mal

The main use of *mal* is in commands, where it implies that the speaker is making more of a suggestion than a demand:

    komm mal her!
    wollen Sie mal meinen Tabak probieren?

Denn

This particle is largely confined to questions. Its meaning is rather hard to make precise, but it gives the question a little more force, with the implication 'in view of this, etc., what about . . . ?' There may thus be a note of contradiction present in an utterance with this particle, and the speaker may be asking about something which does not quite conform to previous assumptions:

    was ist denn das?
    haben Sie denn auch schon selbst mit ihm gesprochen?

Schon

The temporal meaning of the adverb *schon* ('already') is not completely absent from its use as a modal particle, but it suggests logical rather than temporal priority. For example, the utterance

    das ist schon wahr

confirms that the truth of the matter is to be assumed for what follows.

What follows may often be a reservation or qualification (aber . . .), in which case *schon* can take on concessive force ('although'). In other cases, the notion of a logical prerequisite can imply the probability or adequacy of the circumstance or action, and thus be reassuring, e.g.:

> er wird schon kommen
> das stimmt schon

In commands, on the other hand, the implication may be one of impatience:

> kommen Sie schon herein!

Eben

This particle resembles *ja* in conforming a previous utterance or assumption, but is somewhat stronger and firmer in its agreement, with the implication 'that's precisely the point':

> das ist es eben, was ich vermeiden will
> ich mache es, weil man es eben machen muß

Wohl

This might be called the presumptive particle. The speaker is anticipating the hearer's response rather than confirming his previous assumptions, and he presumes that the hearer will agree. This implies probability, but also an element of conjecture:

> Sie kommen wohl auch mit
> er war wohl krank damals

Etwa

If *wohl* conveys probability, *etwa* suggests possibility. It is generally used in questions which are sounding out possibilities rather than making presumptions:

> willst du etwa mitkommen?
> sollte es etwa nicht größer sein?

Auch

As a modal particle *auch* retains something of the 'additive' implication of its full meaning 'also', since it is used in utterances which follow up, or reassert, a previous statement or assumption, either by way of confirmation or contradiction, or as an explanation:

das hat er auch gesagt
ich habe es auch gar nicht gemacht

The above particles are the most important ones, though there are others. No attempt has been made to be exhaustive either in the list of particles or in the discussion of their uses.

MODAL PARTICLES AND GERMAN INTONATION

From the above examples and the brief accompanying explanations, it will be evident that the particles add an implication to an utterance which is rather different from the 'content' of the utterance in the narrow sense. The role of the particles is *to relate the utterance to its context*, and especially to the expectations or assumptions present in this context as a result of previous utterances.

It is instructive to examine the relationship between the modal particles and intonation. Since both of these are concerned not with the content of the utterance as such but rather with its communicative significance in its context, there would appear to be some affinity between them, and we might expect to find a regular relationship between them such that certain particles might automatically entail the use of a specific intonation pattern.

Such regular relationships do not seem to exist, however, and a closer examination of the meaning of the particles will reveal why. Though both intonation and the particles relate the utterance to its context, they do so in rather different ways, and their meanings are of different kinds and do not really overlap. The particles are much more specific in their implications, and are more concerned with linking the content of successive utterances than with the purely communicative dimension that we encountered with intonation. Thus *doch*, for example, suggests a contradiction of a previous assumption and *wohl* a presumption, but neither tells us whether the contradiction or presumption are to be interpreted as assertions or appeals, or whether they are new communicative points or not. There is thus no restriction on the patterns that can be used with either:

das `macht doch nichts
das ´macht doch nichts
Sie kommen wohl `auch mit
Sie kommen wohl ´auch mit

Nor do the particles restrict where the nucleus may fall:

das ˈmacht doch nichts
ˈdas macht doch nichts
das macht doch ˈnichts

Intonation and modal particles are thus in principle independent features of utterances. Nevertheless it is possible to find some relationships between them, however inconsistent these relationships may be. Firstly, it will be observed that some of these particles tend to occur in specific types of sentence – questions or commands – and since there is also a tendency for different sentence types to occur with specific intonation patterns there is evidently the possibility of a relationship, in 'normal' cases, at least. Thus, *denn* occurs mostly in questions, and will often be found with a rising intonation pattern in questions without a question word:

ist er denn geˊkommen?

But it is clear that the relationship is very indirect, since questions with a question word, which generally have a falling pattern, have a fall even if *denn* is present:

was ist denn ˈdas?

Another way in which the particles and the intonation patterns may be related is in terms of their 'strength'. Some of the particles *strengthen* an utterance in the sense of making it more lively or more emphatic, while others *weaken* the utterance in the sense of giving it a milder, more conciliatory tone. In the former category come *doch* and *denn*, in the latter *mal*, *schon*, and *wohl*. Since 'strength' and 'weakness' of a similar kind may also be expressed by intonation, for example in the overall range or height of the pattern, we would expect to find that utterances with 'strong' particles would be uttered with a 'stronger' intonation, and utterances with 'weak' particles would be uttered with a 'weaker' intonation. Thus an utterance with *doch* might well have a more forceful intonation than a corresponding one with *wohl*. This correspondence may well be valid, but, as with all such cases, it is neither obligatory nor consistent, and *doch* and *wohl* may occur with a 'weaker' and 'stronger' intonation respectively.

We must thus conclude that intonation and modal particles are two essentially different features of utterances. They may have a certain relationship in their functions, and may collaborate in giving significance to an utterance, but they remain independent.

GERMAN MODAL PARTICLES AND ENGLISH INTONATION

The above conclusion is also important for the English-speaking learner, since it has been claimed that German modal particles may in their functions correspond to, and therefore 'replace', English intonation patterns. It will be evident from the discussion of the roles of the particles that such an equation of functions is not really valid. Nevertheless we can examine briefly the relationships, in particular with regard to the two patterns of English that have no direct counterpart in German: the low rise and the rise–fall–rise.

As we saw in chapter 10, the English low rise frequently has a 'softening' or encouraging implication; we may therefore perhaps relate it to the use of 'mal', 'schon', or 'wohl', according to the specific context, as in the following examples:

> come ˏhere ; komm mal `her!
> it'll be all ˏright ; es wird schon ´gehen
> it's ˏpossible ; das ist wohl `möglich

But such equivalences are certainly not the only ones, and it would be misleading to treat these as faithful translations. A similar situation arises with the English rise–fall–rise, which often conveys the implication of a reservation. There is really no German particle which could be said to have this connotation, though occasional parallels may be found. The particle 'zwar', for example, may be found to correspond to the rise–fall–rise in concessive sentences:

> it's ˜big / but not very `beautiful
> es ist zwar ´groß / aber nicht sehr `schön

But even in this case the function of the intonation is not really like that of 'zwar'. In a sequence of intonation groups like this, the rise–fall–rise is simply serving to link the intonation groups in a particular way; it does not in itself contain the concessive element of 'zwar'.

In short, therefore, although the learner must certainly attempt to achieve command of the modal particles if he is to have the communicative ability of the native speaker, there is no straightforward way in which he can 'convert' his English intonation patterns into German particles.

Summary of Notation

/	division between intonation groups	
bold type	location of the nucleus: **heu**te	

Nuclear patterns:

`	basic fall	`heute
˝	high fall	˝heute
ˎ	low fall	ˎheute
ˆ	basic rise-fall	ˆheute
˜	wide rise-fall	˜heute
ˬ	narrow rise-fall	ˬheute
´	basic rise	´heute
ˇ	fall-rise	ˇheute
ˏ	narrow rise	ˏheute
⁻	basic level	⁻heute
=	high level	=heute

Heads:

ˈ	high head	ˈheute
ˌ	low head	ˌheute
‖	rising head	‖heute

Further Reading

To extend their knowledge of German intonation readers may wish to consult other published works on the subject. They must, however, be warned that these works are extremely varied in their approach and often differ considerably, both from one another and from the present book, in the conclusions that they reach. Furthermore, work in English on German intonation is extremely limited. The following list contains some of the major contributions only; most of them contain references to further published work in this field.

1. GERMAN INTONATION

M. L. Barker, *A handbook of German intonation for university students,* Cambridge, 1925. The first and hitherto the only book-length work in English dealing with German intonation from the point of view of the English-speaking learner. Inevitably, in the half-century since its publication a great deal more has become known about German intonation, but the book is still usable.

O. von Essen, *Grundzüge der hochdeutschen Satzintonation*, Ratingen, 1956. A standard work on German intonation, which describes some of the basic patterns.

W. G. Moulton, *The Sounds of English and German.* Chicago, 1962. One chapter contains a brief comparison of German and American English intonation, but uses a very different descriptive framework from the present book.

J. L. M. Trim, "Tonetic Stress marks for German", in D. Abercrombie *et al.* (eds.), *In Honour of Daniel Jones.* London, 1964, pp. 374–83. A brief article which presents an analysis of German intonation and a useful way of transcribing it.

A. V. Isačenko & H.-J. Schädlich, *A model of standard German intonation*. Janua Linguarum, Series Practica 113, The Hague, 1970. A theoretical book which gives a rather different view of German intonation from the present work.

E. Stock & Ch. Zacharias, *Deutsche Satzintonation*, Leipzig, 1973. A practical workbook using the approach of Isačenko and Schädlich.

P. A. D. MacCarthy: *The pronunciation of German*, Oxford, 1975. Contains a short but useful chapter on intonation.

J. Pheby, *Intonation und Grammatik im Deutschen*, Berlin, 1975. A theoretical work which applies the descriptive framework of Michael Halliday to German intonation.

—— "Phonologie: Intonation", chapter 6 of K. E. Heidolph, W. Flämig & W. Motsch (eds.), *Grundzüge einer deutschen Grammatik*, Berlin, 1981. The same approach as the foregoing, but revised and more readable.

2. ENGLISH INTONATION

Published work on English intonation is far more extensive and more diverse than work on German. A British and an American approach can be distinguished. Standard works in the British tradition include the following:

L. E. Armstrong and I. C. Ward, *A handbook of English intonation*. Cambridge, 1926. A book published about the same time as M. L. Barker's work on German, and to which the same reservations apply.

H. E. Palmer, *English intonation with systematic exercises*, Cambridge, 1922. A slightly earlier work than that of Armstrong and Ward, but somewhat more sophisticated.

M. Schubiger, *English intonation, its form and function*, Tübingen, 1958. Written by a German phonetician, this book has many comments on the differences between English and German intonation.

R. Kingdon, *The groundwork of English intonation*, London, 1958. A very detailed analysis.

J. D. O'Connor and G. F. Arnold, *Intonation of colloquial English*, London, 1961; 2nd edn. 1973. A current standard pedagogical work.

M. A. K. Halliday, *Intonation and grammar in British English*, The Hague, 1967. A theoretical work by one of the most influential scholars in the field of English intonation.

—— *A course in spoken English: intonation*. Oxford, 1970. A workbook based on the foregoing.

A standard work in the American tradition is:

K. L. Pike, *Intonation of American English*. Ann Arbor, 1945.

3. MODAL PARTICLES

Two articles which discuss the relationship between English intonation and German modal particles are:

M. Schubiger, "English intonation and German modal particles – a comparative study", *Phonetica* 12, 1965, pp. 65–84. Also in D. Bolinger (ed.), *Intonation*, Harmondsworth, 1972, pp. 175--93.

—— "English intonation and German modal particles II – a comparative study", in L. R. Waugh and C. H. van Schooneveld (eds.), *The melody of language*, Baltimore, 1980, pp. 279–98.

Index

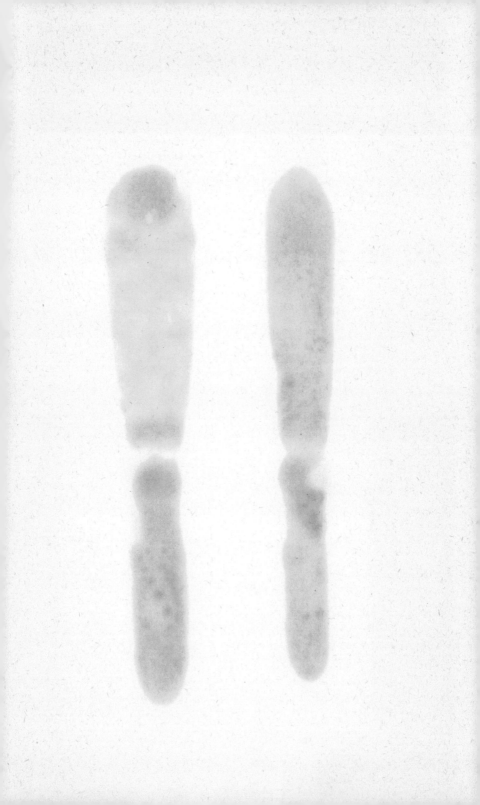

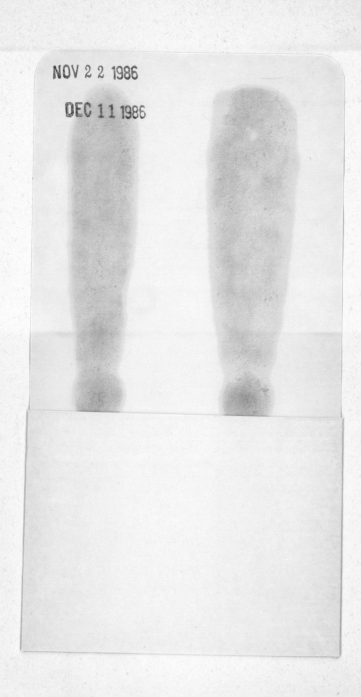